Joy Mawby grew up in Camberley, Surrey, became a teacher and, later, a headteacher.

Throughout her career, she encouraged children with their writing and in the performing arts. She wrote and produced numerous plays for her students.

On retirement, she moved to Anglesey and had time to give to her own writing. She has had several plays performed locally and her first book, '*Footsteps to Freedom*', was published in 2009.

She has two children, three very creative grandchildren and two dogs who keep her fit.

Author website: www.joymawby.co.uk

BROKEN WARRIOR

This book is dedicated to Dziadek and my mother, who was his friend.

Joy Mawby

BROKEN WARRIOR

With ~~best~~ wishes

Joy Mawby

AUSTIN & MACAULEY

A CIP catalogue record for this title is available from the British Library.

ISBN 9781849630870

www.austinmacauley.com

First Published (2012)
Austin & Macauley Publishers Ltd.
25 Canada Square
Canary Wharf
London
E14 5LB

Printed & Bound in Great Britain

I acknowledge my sincere gratitude to:

Konstanty Władisław Dzierżek for teaching me so much.

Konstanty's daughter for trusting me to tell her father's story.

Kay Middlemiss and Vivien Thomas for painstakingly editing my manuscript and for making many helpful suggestions.

Robert Lovell for his computer expertise which he used to help with the reproduction of the photographs, the cover, and with the creation of my website.

John Vesligaj for the loan of valuable books to aid my research.

Danuta Łopacinska, Dziadek's friend, who knows firsthand, about life in pre-war Poland, and who helped me to understand the background to Dziadek's story.

The Amlwch Writing Group for their encouragement.

Madge Robinson and many readers of my first book, *Footsteps to Freedom,* who urged me to write *Broken Warrior.*

Ann Donlan for her advice and expertise.

Contents

Contents 12

Introduction 15

Adventures in English 17

1920 22

Spring 1924 25

Summer 1924 34

Fungus Frenzy 39

Country Pursuits 44

1928 – August 1939 48

Buried Treasure 51

August 1939 – August 1941 55

Transcript of Deposition 61

September 1941 65

September 1941 continued 73

September – October 1941 79

October 1941 88

Shooting Ducks 96

November – December 1941 99

Two Festivals and a Walk 112

January 1942 119

February – Spring 1942 123

Letters 129

Medals and Ribbons... 131

A Mascot and Man's Best Friend 134

Anna.. 139

A Camp and a Batman... 145

The House on the Corner... 151

Postscript 160

Appendix 1, 1920, The Russo-Polish War................. 161

Appendix 2, The Lead-up to The Yalta Conference and Beyond. 162

Glossary of Names, People and Places..................... 165

Bibliography 171

Introduction

In 1997, a ninety-six year old Polish man, Konstanty Władysław Dzierżek, asked me to give him lessons so that he could improve his English.

As our lessons progressed, I learned a great deal about his extraordinary life and times.

After his death, in 1998, I was given access to his memoirs, some letters and documents.

This book is the result of my attempt to put together the various pieces of evidence and write the life story of a remarkable man.

There is a list of people and places in the Glossary which is after Appendix 2.

Adventures in English

'You teacher?'

'Yes.'

'You learn me English please.'

That's how it begins. He is ninety-six years old and has lived in England for over fifty years without picking up more than a smattering of English. Now a widower, he's moved from London to a new life in Cheshire and has decided it's time to learn. He has chosen me to be his teacher. He's a Polish exile and a war hero and he's staring at me with a fierce expression. I know I can't refuse. This is the man who I come to know as 'Dziadek' (pronounced Jadek). It means 'Grandfather'.

Each day we sit together on the settee, his photograph albums by his side and my Polish dictionary by mine. He chooses a photograph, peers at it through a magnifying glass and tries to talk to me about it in his broken English, often assisted by his daughter, Danka, and prompted by my questions. I listen carefully and make the odd note or two. Then, while he drinks coffee and rests, I write the nub of the story in large letters on the back of a cut-up roll of wallpaper. Next I read it slowly and clearly to him. Finally he reads it to me twice before I fasten it to the back of the door with blu-tak. This is so that he can read it as often as he wishes before we meet for another session. Each lesson starts with reading through the previous day's story and any others he fancies.

I'm not sure that Dziadek's spoken English improves very much but his face lights up when it's lesson time. He laughs aloud at some of the recollections that are prompted by the photos. He loves to teach me too – about life in a country manor and the Polish names of fungi, fish and game birds.

Once I asked him why he didn't learn to speak English when he first came here after the war. He didn't try to answer, just shrugged and turned away. I discover, from his family, that he didn't bother because he thought he would soon be returning to Poland. He and his compatriots were convinced that their hero, General Anders, would lead them back to Poland to a glorious victory over the occupying Soviet army. At last a free Homeland would be re-established.

By the mid-fifties it was obvious that there would be no return. Then Dziadek was depressed and too angry to attempt to learn English. He felt let down by the Allies. He had fought hard not just for Poland but for the whole of the 'free world' and now he was stranded in a foreign place, unable to return to the land he loved. However, by the mid-sixties he seems to have decided it was worth trying to communicate with his neighbours so he enrolled in an English evening class which was held in the local school. He didn't say much about it at home but set out, each Wednesday, his book under his arm.

When a Mr Bagaj, a Ukrainian friend, asked him about the lessons he was reticent and was not at all pleased when he arrived one day to find that his friend had joined the class. Mr Bagaj reported to Dziadek's wife, Anna, afterwards, 'He was the only man there. The teacher is a young and pretty lady and all of the other students are beautiful au pair girls. They cluster round him, help him with his work and one even brought in some little cakes for him.'

In spite of Mr Bagaj, Dziadek continued to attend the classes until the day when he made the mistake of reading his homework aloud to his family. 'My Garden.' He paused as if proud of his newly acquired skill. Then he went on, 'In my garden I have plenty smelly peas and...' The family's laughter drowned the rest of the sentence. Deeply offended, Dziadek threw down his book. He didn't have another English lesson until 1997.

Dziadek's name is Konstanty Władysław Nieczuja Dzierżek. He was born in 1901, cared for by a Russian nanny and educated, at first, by a German governess. He was sent away to school at the age of seven.

I discover this, one day, when he has his photo album open at a snowy picture. 'Delamere' he says.

'Delamere?'

'By Chester,' he explains, and I remember hearing that he was Commandant of a Polish resettlement camp there after the war. I look more closely at the picture. It's dated 1947.

Dziadek with his wife and daughter.

'I remember the winter of 1947,' I say. 'It was very cold. Our school was closed down because the pipes were frozen.' I accompany my reply with exaggerated shivers.

'You think 1947 cold?'

'Yes, very cold. My answer obviously delights him. He laughs and points to the snowy photo again.

'Not cold. Moscow cold. Running in snow, no clothes, early morning cold.'

'Why would anyone in Moscow do that?'

Cadet Corps School. It school for army and page boys.' This seems such a bizarre concept that I decide to do some research.

First I ask Danka what she knows about it. 'Not very much,' she says. 'I know my father went to boarding school when he was seven. The discipline seems to have been pretty tough. He did tell me that the Tsar's son was there at the same time as he was. He says he sang a solo to the Tsarina, when she visited the school once, but he's more or less tone deaf so I don't know what she thought of it.'

On the internet I discover that the school Dziadek attended in Moscow was one of several similar schools, situated in some of the main cities in Russia. They were schools for boys of noble birth. Entry criteria were high. Applicants were tested on mathematics and had to be familiar with two languages. The aim of the schools was to turn out officials of the royal household, civil servants and officer cadets. Students learned science, mathematics, literature, history, law, foreign languages, horsemanship, fencing and dance. Graduates of the Cadet Corps Schools, where honour, altruism and modesty were highly prized, were among the most distinguished military leaders and statesmen of their day. The Tsar and Tsarina often visited the schools. They inspected everything, including the quality of the food.

Then I remember hearing Anna once say how cross she got because Dziadek never picked up his discarded clothes.

'Just steps out of them and leaves them on the floor for me to pick up,' she'd grumbled. 'It all started at that school he went to. He had a batman there to tidy up after him.'

I think of all this as we start the lesson the next day. Here I am with one of the graduates of a famous and exclusive Moscow school, trying to teach him to speak English. Suddenly I feel embarrassed by my infant school methods. But Dziadek is smiling and showing me a photograph and I know that there can be no turning back.

Later I ask him to tell me more about his school. 'What did you do each day?' He thinks for a moment, stretches his arms to the front then to the side.

'Early – exercise then run outside like Spartan.' As far as I can understand, the students came back from the run to a communal steam bath and cold dip. After breakfast they did academic work in classrooms. In the afternoons there was drill or fencing, or horsemanship. Later, after a period of recreation, homework had to be done before bedtime. They must have slept very well.

He's tired at the end of our lesson. He sits back and closes his eyes, but I don't think he's asleep. I wonder what he's thinking. Has his mind gone back to earlier days?

1920

'Don't ask questions. Just make sure you're there. If you're not you'll be in serious trouble – and I mean really big trouble.'

Those words from one of the union bosses were still ringing in my ears the next day as his officious colleague shouted, 'Get into line! Straighten up! Eyes this way!' Resignedly we shuffled, straightened and looked to the front.

'The sooner we get this right, the sooner they'll let us go,' whispered my neighbour and Polish friend, Adam. At last the man was satisfied and I had time to look around. I saw a motley selection of 'workers' arranged round a central podium in the town square. I was among the Railway Union workers and was helping to support a banner proclaiming 'PROLETARIANS OF ALL LANDS UNITE'. Two brass bands arrived, led by soldiers of artillery and cavalry regiments. Each was trying to outdo the other in renditions of loud patriotic marching music. These were followed by members of the Komsomol (Young Communists), behind whom marched youngsters from schools and orphanages. They carried a banner which I couldn't quite see. Then they turned to face us, on the other side of the square, and I saw 'WARSAW IS OURS' in large red letters. I couldn't help my sharp intake of breath. I daren't look at Adam. Other banners had arrived, exhorting us to 'GO FORWARD TOGETHER IN VICTORY' and to remember there is 'STRENGTH IN UNITY'.

News of the Bolshevik's moves against Poland had reached us weeks ago and even a whisper that Warsaw had fallen. We hadn't believed that. But if this was actually a parade of victory… Despair swept over me. I desperately wanted to be part of the Polish Resistance against the invaders and here I was, participating in a Soviet Rally to celebrate the overthrow of our beloved capital city. How had this come about? In truth, I could hardly believe it myself.

The fact was, my father, an expert in railway design and employed by the Tsarist Government, had brought my mother to live in Russia shortly before I was born. Father died when I was ten, I finished my education and then my family (Mother, my brother, two sisters) and I were caught up in the turbulence of the First World War. Before that had ended the Russian Revolution and Civil War were upon us. Our house was requisitioned and we ended up sharing a humble dwelling with several other families. In the pervading political climate, the only thing to do was to keep as low a profile as possible and wait for an opportunity to return to Poland. Currently we were prevented from doing so by Soviet officialdom. I had needed to find work to support the family. As I was known at the local railway office I had managed to secure a position working in the forest, helping to construct the Moscow to Belarus section of the railway. As a railway worker I had no option but to join the Rail Workers' Union.

At last, at midday, three dignitaries walked on to the podium. Suddenly a soldier on a badly winded horse galloped past and stopped in front of them. He dismounted and one of the men on the platform leant forward to hear what he had to say. The soldier whispered something and then led his horse away. The dignitaries conferred and frowned and conferred again. Then they left the podium. There was no explanation. They simply went down the steps, walked past the expectant groups and into the town hall. A moment later a man appeared, running. He whispered to one of the organisers who called the other officials over. They huddled together, shrugging and gesticulating. We couldn't hear what they were saying but all at once, without looking at us, they turned and walked away. When they had gone, the messenger spoke to the two band leaders who silenced their musicians mid-song and then led them and their followers back the way they had come. Finally the cavalry and artillery regiments marched quietly away. We and the Soviet organisations were left, still holding our banners. A hubbub ensued – everyone asking what had happened but no *answers were forthcoming. Banners were dropped and the crowd dispersed slowly.*

My fellow Poles and I hung back, and talked quietly.
'What do you think has happened?' murmured Adam.
Tadek laughed. 'I think that there has been no "Glorious Victory" after all.'
'I'm sure there hasn't,' Stefan added. 'In fact, I'm inclined to believe there's been a Glorious Defeat. I feel sure that Warsaw hasn't fallen to the Soviets. I'll go even further and declare that the Red Army has been well and truly beaten.' I could only agree. We laughed and gave a muted cheer. Then we laid our banners on the ground beside the others and, with a last look back at the sea of propaganda which now surrounded the platform, we laughed again and went our separate ways.

For further information on some of the events which are mentioned here, see Appendix 1.

Spring 1924

Even now I can hear the angry voice, the voice of that pig-like Soviet official who was Governor of the Gubispolkom (Provincial Office).

'Get out of here,' he shouted. 'Why are you bothering me with your petty requests? I don't deal with passports. Go to the Ispolkom (Town Council Office). Waste their time not mine.'

'I've already been to the Ispolkom. I was told to come here.'

'Liar!' shrieked the Governor. 'Get out before I call someone to throw you out.'

Outside in the street, I stood still and considered what to do. It was Thursday, 25th April 1924. My family and I had to be out of Russia by 1st May – six days away. After that the border would be closed. Non-Soviets who remained would lose everything, possibly even their lives. I had applied for visas and updated passports for us all, months ago, but had only just received them. My sisters, as minors, were named on my mother's passport but Henry had reached the age of eighteen while we were waiting for the visas to arrive and his name was not included. Without a valid passport, he couldn't travel across the border to Poland. On realising this I had gone straight to the Town Council Offices in Rżew where we resided, and was directed to the Provincial Office at Twer. I'd travelled there by train and was now no further forward. With time running out, I realised that the Polish Consul in Moscow was my only hope. I ran back to the station and just managed to catch the night train.

'I understand your predicament,' said the Consul as I faced him over his desk the next morning. 'However, I regret that I am unable to help you. Granting passports is outside my jurisdiction.

You must apply to the Soviet Commissar for Foreign Affairs and I'm afraid it will not be possible for you to obtain even an interview with him before Wednesday. These things take time and everything closes down over the weekend.'

'Wednesday?' I thought. 'Wednesday is the last day we can leave the country.'

As I retraced my steps I felt a light touch on my shoulder and, fearing trouble, I turned to face a smart and distinguished-looking lady. She said nothing but indicated, with her eyes, that I should follow her into an empty room. She closed the door and spoke softly. 'I work for the Consul and overheard your conversation with him. If you give me your word of honour that what I tell you will remain a secret I may be able to help you.'

Astonished, I could only stammer, 'I give you my word.'

'The Commissar's private secretary is one of ours. I mean she works quietly and secretly to help Polish people. If you go to her, very discreetly, she may well be able to help you. Approach her carefully because she will be very wary of you. Her office is up one flight of stairs. It's the first door on the left that you come to.'
Before I could thank this Good Samaritan she'd opened the door and slipped out, leaving me to check that no-one was looking and then follow her directions. Hope surged as I ran up the stairs.

A pleasant-faced young woman was standing at a filing cabinet when I opened the door and entered at her invitation. She looked at me, enquiringly. As I explained my business I saw a frown pass over her face. 'I don't know why you've come to me. I'm afraid I can't help you... I could make you an appointment to see the Commissar at the end of next week. Beyond that, I can't be of service to you.'

I took a deep breath, looked into her eyes, and very deliberately said, 'I know you could help if you wanted to.' The colour drained from her face and she swayed so that she had to grip the filing cabinet.

'Please don't be afraid,' I said quickly. 'I swear on my mother's life that I will never utter one word of what passes between us now, whether or not you choose to help me.'

'Who told you I might help?' she asked.

'I'm sorry but I can't reveal that. You don't really expect me to, do you?'

She shook her head with a little smile. 'I'll do what I can,' she said quietly.

I had a sudden idea. 'Does the Commissar read everything he signs?' I asked.

'No. Usually he tells me in the morning which documents he wants me to prepare. I put them on his desk each afternoon. He simply signs them and I make sure they reach their destinations.'

'Would it be possible for you to write a document, ordering the Gubispolkom in Twer to issue a passport to Henry Dzierżek immediately, as he's been deleted from his mother's passport on reaching the age of eighteen?'

There was a long pause. I felt sure she could hear my heart beating as I waited for her reply. At last, 'All right. I'll try but I can't promise anything. I'm sure you're aware of the consequences for me and for your family if this goes wrong.'

'I am. Thank you,' was all I could say.

'Come back at four o'clock. Don't knock on my door. Wait in the corridor. If all is well I'll come out to you when it's safe. Now go.' Thanking her again, I went downstairs and out of the building.

I wandered round the town for five hours. Sometimes I was hopeful and imagined all would be well. At other times I envisaged our having to leave Henry behind when we returned to Poland. Worse still I saw our entire family being arrested and thrown into prison alongside the Commissar's secretary. I could neither eat nor drink and the hours crept by. At last it was almost 4 o'clock and I re-entered the building, checking for unusual activity, police or guards. All seemed unchanged. I mounted the stairs and walked the length of the empty corridor, trying not to look at the secretary's door. I walked up and down for several minutes and then the door opened and she saw me. Her face lit up. She walked towards me and slipped into my hand a long white envelope. She shook her head slightly to prevent me from speaking. 'Good luck,' she whispered.

All I could do was shape my lips into a silent 'Thank you'. Then she was gone.

I reached the Gubispolkom, in Twer, the next morning. The building was deserted except for a drunken caretaker sitting by the door.

'Ish a holiday,' he slurred. 'Ish a holiday an I'm in charge.'

'I need to see the Governor,' I said. 'I have an important paper for him from the Commissar for Foreign Affairs in Moscow. Go to his home and fetch him'

'Ish no good. Ish a holiday. Shairman snot here.' It seemed hopeless but I decided to try bribery. 'I'll give you a bottle of vodka if you go and tell the Governor that there is a very important message for him and he must come to his office to receive it. Will you do that?' His befuddled brain grasped the promise of vodka and he stood up unsteadily.

'I'll keep an eye on the building for you while you're gone.' I said. 'As the message is so important, I'd better wait in the Governor's office. Unlock it for me.'

He obeyed without question. I sat at the Governor's desk and asked him, 'What are you going to say to the Governor?'

'Very important visitor from Moscow shere...Commissar...'

'That's fine. Hurry now. Don't hang around.' I sat still and planned my speech to the Governor.

Surprisingly quickly I heard loud voices in the corridor. I leaned back in the chair, picked up a piece of paper from the desk and pretended to study it. The Governor burst in. When he saw me his red face turned purple.

'How dare you?' he shrieked. 'Get out of my office. You'll be sorry for this.' And, screaming at the caretaker who was standing behind him, 'Get the police. This man is trespassing.' I signalled to the caretaker to stay where he was and stood up.

I held the document from the Commissar up so that the Governor could see the signature and I shouted back at him, 'It's *you who'll be sorry. How dare you treat me in this way? I have been speaking to the Commissar for Foreign Affairs in Moscow. He gave me this document to give to you and you dare to threaten me with the police?'*

As soon as the Governor saw the signature a transformation took place. His knees seemed to buckle and he sank into a chair as his purple face took on an ashen hue.

'Tovarish (Comrade) Dzierżek, I didn't know... of course I want to help you... but how can I? You can see that there is no typist here and no cashier either... and the passports are in the safe...What can I do?'

'You can summon the staff you need at once!' I insisted. 'If you don't, I'll be forced to inform the Commissar for Foreign Affairs of your unwillingness to obey his orders.'

'Of course, at once Sir Konstantin Vladyslavovich. Don't be angry. I will do as you say. I will arrange everything. They will be here shortly. You must be hungry and thirsty after your journey. A samovar?' He shouted at the considerably sobered caretaker to fetch the necessary personnel and then fetched a samovar and some small biscuits. As we drank the hot sweet tea he made many excuses as to why he had been unable to provide a passport when I first saw him. He was a frightened man.

By lunchtime the passport was in my hands. I managed to catch a goods train to Torzek and another to Rżew, where my anxious family awaited my return. How they laughed at the story of the Governor as we sat down for a meal together.

We left Rżew and Russian soil by train, on 1ˢᵗ May.

I stopped, for a moment, on the platform of Minsk Station to look at the new engine which was being attached to our train. Suddenly, out of the crowd an emaciated, ragged Polish woman emerged holding, by the arm, a boy of about ten. She halted next to me and whispered fiercely in my ear, 'Please, I beg you, take my son with you to Poland. For his sake and mine, I beseech you.' I looked around quickly. No-one seemed to have noticed her speaking to me. I beckoned her in the direction of a deserted parcel depot, which would give us some shelter.

'Why do you ask me to do this, madam?' I asked softly.

'My husband worked in Minsk as a bookkeeper,' she told me. 'Seven years ago he disappeared without trace. I have searched everywhere for him, hospitals, jails, asylums – everywhere. I now feel sure that he is dead. As I am Polish it is impossible for me to get work here. My passport was stolen some time ago so I can't leave the country. My son and I are starving and can only live by begging. Recently a Soviet man, a member of the Party, has been showing an interest in me. I think he will marry me if I so wish and then I'll have a proper home and food. Please don't despise me for this. I must either go with him or die.'

'Madam, it's not for me to judge you but why do you want me to take your son? Has he a passport?'

'No he hasn't. But do please try to get him to Poland. I can't bear the thought of his growing up a Communist. I don't care for myself but he is my only child and I must do what's best for him. My mother and brother live in Warsaw. I think they have moved and I haven't got their new address but I'm sure you'll be able to find them.' She pushed a piece of paper into my hand. 'This is their surname. Please, please help me.'

I thought quickly. It would probably be possible for us to hide the boy amongst our luggage when we crossed the Polish border. I looked at him and asked him his name.

'Janek, sir,'

'Well Janek, will you promise to do exactly as I say?'

'I promise sir.'

'Then you may come with us. We must hurry now because the train is about to leave.'

The poor woman clung to her son for a moment and then, with tears running down her face, pushed him towards me.

'Go, my darling and may God bless you, and you sir…' She could say no more. The boy bit his lip to stop his tears and I hurried him away towards our part of the train, without a backward glance.

My mother was not pleased when I returned to the carriage and explained Janek's presence. 'Kostek, whatever were you thinking? You should never have promised his mother. How can we be responsible for another child? You've had trouble enough getting us this far. If the boy's discovered we'll all be thrown into prison.'

'Then we'll just have to make sure he isn't discovered, won't we? The deed is done and I'm sure it's the right deed. Janek's mother is as concerned for his future as you were for Henry's when it seemed we wouldn't be able to get a passport for him.'

This silenced my mother who looked thoughtful and then handed a piece of bread and sausage to the hungry boy.

We stopped at the Russian border and our papers were checked. We were all nervous as the Soviet official looked into our carriage but fortunately he scarcely glanced at our little pile of shabby luggage. Janek lay quite still beneath it. The train moved off slowly and he was safe. I helped him out and my mother hugged him. He'd become 'one of us' and we were now in our Homeland.

Our first stop in Poland was at Stolpcow. I knew I'd now have to admit to smuggling Janek over the border so I took him with me to the Customs Office. I showed the official the family's passports and then explained to him how the boy came to be travelling with us.

He frowned. 'I'll speak to the lad alone. Wait outside.'

'Why? I've told you the truth. Surely you wouldn't expect us to leave him to goodness knows what fate in Russia?'

'Please do as I say. Wait outside my office.' I saw I had no alternative so I obeyed with bad grace. After a few minutes the official called me in. He was smiling.

'I had to make sure you hadn't taken the boy against his will, sir. His story matches yours and I'll issue a temporary passport for him, if you'll undertake to care for him until you locate his family.'

'He can live with us in Warsaw while we search for his relatives,' I answered. 'We'll do all in our power to find them. If we can't, I'll become his legal guardian.' The official nodded his approval and handed me a passport for Janek.

'Now take your luggage to the shed, please,' he said. 'The customs officers there will check it.'

When our meagre luggage was spread before the custom officers my mother gave a cry.

'Konstanty, how could you? We could all have been shot if the Soviets had found those!' She was pointing at the two hunting rifles I had hidden among my clothes. It had been a risk but one worth taking. The officers were laughing and one clapped me on the back.

'Well done. You tricked those wretched Soviets but I'm afraid we'll have to confiscate them until you get a gun licence. You can get one in Warsaw. Bring it to us and we'll ensure these beautiful weapons are returned to you.'

In Warsaw we were to stay with my uncle, Alexander Borowski. He greeted us with enthusiasm and made us all very welcome. Over the next few days we bought some decent clothes and I obtained a gun licence and travelled back to Stolpcow to claim the rifles. When I held them in my hands, once more I was furious.

'Who's been firing my guns?' I demanded. 'They're dirty. They were absolutely clean when I handed them to you.' The official looked sheepish and shrugged his shoulders nervously. My raised voice brought the boss into the room – the man who had provided Janek's passport.

'Someone has fired both of my rifles,' I told him. 'Whoever it was hasn't even had the courtesy to clean them.'

'I do apologise,' he replied and turned to the nervous individual who had handed them to me. 'Take these outside and clean them thoroughly.' And turning to me, 'Again, I apologise. Come and drink tea with me while your guns are cleaned.'

When I got back to uncle's house, I found Janek and a stranger waiting for me in the drawing room. In my absence, Henry had managed to trace Janek's uncle and send him a message. Now he had come to take the boy home with him.

'How can I ever thank you?' he said. 'You ran a great risk and we'll always be grateful.'

'It's only what anyone would have done.'

'I don't think so. It was an exceptionally kind and courageous thing to do. I'm a minister in the government and if there is ever anything I can do for you, you have only to ask.'

'Thank you.'

'Janek's grandmother and I will care for him for as long as necessary but I intend to instigate a search, in Minsk, to try to find my sister and bring her back to Poland.'

He rose to go and shook my hand warmly. Janek gravely extended his hand too. I took it in both of mine.

'Good luck,' I said and, as I showed them out of the house, I felt a deep sense of contentment.

Summer 1924

I felt I deserved a holiday after the difficulties of getting out of Soviet Russia. 'You're welcome to stay in the forest house, if you wish,' my uncle said. I loved his big country house which was near the famous beauty spot, 'The Queen of the Waters', so I accepted his offer with alacrity.

For a while I relaxed. I fished, swam, gathered berries, and best of all, found the season's first fungi. I cooked them and shared them with two students who were staying in the house. Chodorowski and Borek were from a local university and engaged in research. They planned to catalogue the flora and fauna of the forest.

'It's a tremendous amount of work,' Borek said to me over our first fungi feast, 'You wouldn't care to give us a hand, would you – for, say, two and a half zlotys a day?' I was very short of cash and jumped at the chance.

After a few days Chodorowski had an idea. He put it to me as we had pre-dinner drinks. 'I say, you're terribly good at all this quartering, naming and counting stuff. How about you doing the field work on your own? That'll leave us free to get on with the piles of theory and paperwork here. It'll speed things up enormously.'

I thoroughly enjoyed working on my own and the arrangement with the students worked harmoniously. An added bonus was the number of edible fungi I found. They made a welcome addition to most of our meals.

All was well until one day when two inspectors from the university arrived, unannounced. Fortunately I was in the house at the time. 'We've come to look at your field work,' said the senior inspector. I saw the panic on the faces of my two co-conspirators and realised that they had no idea exactly where in the forest I'd been working for the last couple of weeks. I stepped in quickly.

'Some of the usual paths have been closed because of re-planting,' I improvised. 'I've been acting as guide to Chodorowski and Borek as it's not always easy to find the way. May I be permitted to act as guide to you now?'

'Indeed you may,' answered the inspector. 'Thank you very much.'

Later, when the satisfied inspectors had departed, Borek grinned at me. 'We reckon you're worth double what we're giving you. Will five zlotys a day suit you?'

Although I was enjoying this interlude I was conscious that I must find employment. My dearest wish was to join the Polish army, so when I heard that the 3rd Regiment Light Infantry was recruiting for their Officer Academy, in Suwalki, I arranged to meet the Adjutant. 'I'm sorry,' he said. 'You're too old to enter the school. Also you haven't done your National Service.' Disappointed, I returned to my uncle's house. As my forest research came to an end, I received an unexpected invitation from family friends, the Krupskis.

We hadn't seen each other since 1917 so there was much rejoicing when I arrived. I felt absolutely at home as I sat down to my first meal with the family. Mr and Mrs Krupski's older daughter, Tala, was a beautiful young woman and a student at Krakow University. Perhaps one day... Talk turned to Mr Krupski's latest assignment. He was a civil engineer and had been contracted to rebuild a wooden bridge over a road.

'It's been damaged – almost demolished – by artillery shells,' he explained. 'In fact the bridge is one of the reasons I suggested we should invite you here. I'm up to my eyes in work and wondered if you would take responsibility for rebuilding it, under my guidance. It would mean sourcing the materials and

supervising the workmen. What do you think?' I was astonished and grateful.

'If you think I'm up to it, I'd be delighted to accept your offer. I promise I won't let you down.'

'I'm sure you won't,' he replied. 'Oh, I almost forgot, I have a motorbike and sidecar you can borrow for getting about.'

Later, in my own bedroom, I remembered Mr Krupski's words '...the bridge is one of the reasons I suggested we should invite you here.' One of the reasons – could the other be so that Tala and I could get to know each other better? I hoped so. Not only was she beautiful, she was highly intelligent and had a sparkling humour which I found irresistible. Of course nothing could happen between us for a long time. At the moment I had no career and she was studying. Still, I must make the most of this opportunity.

Each day I set out for work, at first with Mr Krupski but later by myself. I learned so much during the next months: how to sink foundations for the bridge, how to choose suitable trees and stone for different parts of the structure, how to make sure the labourers were thorough in their work and the order in which each phase of the building must be done. However, all the time I was aware that, interesting as this employment was, it was only temporary and it certainly wasn't what I wanted to do for the rest of my working life.

Leisure time was enjoyable. Tala loved to ride on the back of the motorbike although her mother didn't really approve. Sometimes there were family picnics and once a dance when Tala and I discovered how well we danced together.

One evening, as we were relaxing in the drawing room, we heard gunfire nearby. We rushed outside. The night was dark and we could see nothing amiss. We heard more shots and I turned to Mr Krupski. 'I think you should take everyone inside and lock the *doors, sir. I'll ride over to the Police Post for information and to see if I can be of any help.'*

'But you'll put yourself in danger,' he argued. 'We could go together.' It was clear to me that he should stay with the family, especially as I was faster on a horse than he. I didn't want the responsibility of another person with me, in the forest, when speed was of the essence. Unfortunately, the motorbike was almost out of fuel, so after further argument and intervention by Mrs Krupski, I set off alone.

The forest was pitch black and, as the wind got up, every movement of the trees and each sound their branches made was magnified. But deep down I was enjoying the frisson, the adventure. I even found myself hoping that I would be called upon to perform some act of valour – that I would be the one to save the Krupskis (particularly Tala) from certain death. But it was not to be.

I reached the road and the Police Post safely. It housed not only ordinary civilian policemen but a detachment of Frontier Guard Police too. The building was locked and barred so I hammered on the door several times. A shutter was thrown open and a voice asked, 'Who's there?'

'I've come from Mr Krupski's house. I...'

'Oh it's you from the bridge, isn't it? I'll be straight down.'

'There's been an attack, by bandits, at the railway station,' the duty policeman explained. 'A patrol has gone to deal with the situation. I'll know more, of course, when they get back.'

'Is there anything I can do to help?' I asked hopefully.

'Thank you, no. It's all under control.'

The Krupskis were relieved to see me back in one piece. Tala came over to me. 'I'm so glad you're safe,' she whispered.

The next day I heard that no-one had been badly hurt in the attack and that the bandits had been caught and money retrieved.

The house seemed dull when Tala had to return to Krakow and the next highlight was the completion of the bridge. Mr Krupski was delighted and remunerated me generously. Better even than that, he brought me a cutting from a newspaper. It was notice that the Army Officer Academy in Warsaw was inviting candidates to apply for places at the college for the next academic year.

I applied for a form straight away, completed and returned it along with my CV. Within a few days I received an invitation to present myself, with a medical certificate, at the Academy. There I would be given the syllabus on which the entry examinations, in two months' time, would be based. There wasn't a moment to lose. I bid a hasty and grateful farewell to the Krupskis and departed for Warsaw.

I studied non-stop for two months, staying at my uncle's town house. Everyone else was on the coast – away from the insufferable heat of the capital. I lived alone, going out in the early morning to buy provisions and keeping cool by taking frequent cold baths. A servant came each weekend to clean the house and deal with the laundry. Apart from seeing her, I lived a hermit's life.

I thought the exam went reasonably well, in spite of my nervousness. However, I hardly dared look at the list of results pinned on the Academy notice board a couple of weeks later. Sick with apprehension, I ran my eyes up the list, starting from the bottom and there it was – my name – fairly near the top. I breathed deeply with relief. At last my training to become an officer in the Polish Army could begin. It had been my ambition since I was a little boy.

On our first day at the Academy our heads were shaved. From that moment, for three years, we worked extremely hard both mentally and physically. Those were the happiest years of my life.

Fungus Frenzy

We are looking at a photograph of a group of smiling people squeezed together in a little handcart. Dziadek points to the girl on the far right.

'This Tala,' he says. 'Very pretty.'

'All the girls are pretty.'

'No. She *very* pretty.'

'You like her?'

He shrugs and smiles, 'I like. Here we go look fungus.'

'Look for fungus – why?' Dziadek looks at me incredulously, as if I have asked a crazy question.

The Fungus Foray
Far left Dziadek. Far right Tala

'Eat, eat!' he smacks his lips.

'You mean mushrooms,' I correct him. You can eat mushrooms. Fungi are poisonous.'

'No, no, no! Lots fungus good for eating too.' He reaches for a book – a guide to fungi – and opens it at random. 'Look this fungus good for eat and this and this.'

'Oh, I didn't know. Sorry.'

'Mushroom is fungus too.' Dziadek is in didactic mode and shows me more edible fungi. Then I turn back to the handcart photo.

'Before war.' Dziadek says as he looks at it again. Danka comes into the room.

'Your fungus hunting didn't stop there, did it Dad? Tell Joy about when you went looking for fungi on Bookham Common and got lost.' Dziadek looks embarrassed.

'No, not then. I tell fungus in Poland.'

The house guests at Dziadek's Uncle Edward's country mansion assembled especially for the fungus season. They set off for the woods before dawn. Each person carried a knife, to cut the fungi, and servants pushed the handcart containing empty baskets and the picnic.

'I good fungus nose,' says Dziadek, touching his large nose and sniffing. 'I smell easy and see quick.'

Once they were in the woods, the sweet new fungi were gathered at speed. They were placed in baskets and loaded into the cart while servants lit a fire, made coffee and prepared breakfast.

'Fungus high in cart,' Dziadek indicates with his hand. 'Best of all is borowik.' In the book he shows me the large brown fungus which is clearly his favourite. 'It...' he kisses his bunched fingers to indicate just how delicious this particular species is.

It seems that high spirits prevailed after breakfast on fungi day. When everything was packed away for the return journey there was 'hide and seek' and horse play. There was singing on the way home too, as the servants pushed the cart with its precious load.

Once back at the house, most of the fungi were put to dry before being bottled. However, some were put aside and in the evening family and friends sat down to a splendid feast of fungi fried in butter with sour cream, onions and paprika.

Dziadek never lost his love of fungi. In England he was an acknowledged expert in the Polish community. People came from far and near to check whether the fungi they had found were safe to eat.

After the war, he lived for a while in Cheshire and he was delighted to find that it was fungus country. His love of fungi once led to an international misunderstanding. He and Anna had been collecting edible fungi of all sorts in Delamere Forest. They found themselves at the edge of the trees, adjacent to a farm. The farmer saw them standing with overflowing baskets and came running over.

'What are you doing? You can't eat that poison,' he cried.

'Poison?' Dziadek was puzzled.

'Trucizna,' translated Anna. Her husband was outraged but Anna tried to explain to the farmer.

'These aren't poisonous. Some fungi are but all of these are good to eat.'

'No, no,' the man protested. 'Look,' he pulled a ten shilling note from his pocket. 'If you're starving use this to buy yourselves some food. If you throw those poisonous things away you can have this money.' Anna declined the kind offer politely. Muttering about starving foreigners with no sense and saying that he wouldn't have them on his conscience because he'd offered them money, the farmer strode away.

When Dziadek was eighty five and living in south London, Danka took him and his close friend, a Polish general who was almost ninety, to Bookham Common, Surrey, on a fungi hunt. Dziadek and the General had been friends since they had attended

41

the Officer Academy together, a lifetime ago. On arrival, the General set off on what looked like a promising path, leaving the other two searching close to the car park. When they had collected two baskets full, Danka said to her father, 'You stay here. I'll take these back to the car and empty them into the box. Then we'll go and see what the General has found.' When Danka returned Dziadek was nowhere to be seen.

She called and searched. She followed the path the General had taken – all to no avail. After an hour she returned to the car, hoping to find them there. No-one. She waited in the car and searched in turn. After about three hours of doing this, she saw a car turn into the car park. A couple got out, carrying a picnic. Danka approached them and explained what had happened.

'We're going to have a snack and a short walk. We'll certainly keep our eyes open for your father and his friend,' said the woman.

'Thank you very much,' responded Danka. 'I'm going to look for a telephone box. I'll phone my mother to explain the situation because she'll be expecting us back at any moment. If you do see them tell them to wait for me here. I won't be long.'

'Don't hang around any longer,' instructed Anna on the phone. 'Go back to the car park once more and if they're not there come home. If we haven't had any news by that time, I suppose we'll have to phone the police.'

The phone was ringing as Danka reached home. Anna answered it. It was an Officer from Guildford police station.

'There's an elderly gentleman here who says he's a general. He doesn't speak much English but he had your phone number on a piece of paper. Do you know him?'

Anna explained what had happened and enquired whether her husband was there too.

'Sorry madam, we've only got the one stray gentleman at present,' answered the Officer. 'But we'll keep a look out for the other. Give me your address, please and we'll return the General to you.' Almost before the conversation had ended, a police car drew up outside the house and a policeman emerged to help Dziadek out. Danka went to meet him.

'He didn't know where he'd been, madam,' said the policeman 'and he didn't know he'd arrived in Kingston, but he did know his address so here he is. You do know him, don't you?'

'He's my father,' said Danka grimly. 'Thank you very much indeed for bringing him home.' To Dziadek, she whispered fiercely, 'And don't you think that I'll ever take you to look for fungi again!'

Country Pursuits

'Palac w Michalowcach.' I have a go at reading aloud the name of a stately home, which is Dziadek's chosen picture of the day. He laughs at my attempt and shows me how it should be pronounced.

Palac W Michalowcach

'Michalowce,' he says. It very big house at Michalowce. Uncle Edward.'

'This is the country house you told me about? The one that belonged to your Uncle Edward, where you used to go for your fungi parties?' I'm incredulous.

'Yes. It 'Dzierżkowice'. House name.'

'From your family name?'

'Yes. It family house. We go in holidays.'

He picks up my felt pen and places it one end of the coffee table. 'This when I go Officer Academy.' He places my pencil at the other end of the table. 'This war.' He waves his hand along the space between pen and pencil. 'Here I go many times to 'Dzierżkowice' for hunt, fish, fungus, party'

Uncle Edward was the head of the Dzierzek clan. He never married and his country mansion was always open to members of the family and their friends. Apart from the fungus forays, there were weeks of hunting wild boar in the surrounding forest, and weekends when Dziadek would bring some of his army friends to shoot wild fowl and to fish in the river and lake. They often went camping for a few days to pursue these country sports. There were also house parties and balls and theatricals when ladies were present to add to the pleasure of the occasion.

'We play with cards too and with chess,' he says. I remember hearing what a formidable bridge player he is, and once when I'd played chess with him, he'd wiped me off the board in less than half a dozen moves.

The drawing room

I gather from what Dziadek says, that in season, the house parties and sporting endeavours took place on many of the estates of his friends as well as at Dzierżkowice. Thus young people in his 'set' moved from one arena of pleasure to another. It's no wonder that he's looking wistfully at another photograph. It shows a group of people sitting stiffly under a painting of a warrior in armour. 'Dzierżkowice', he says.

'This looks like the drawing room,' I say. In fact, if it weren't for the people in the picture, it would resemble many a stately home I've visited.

'Yes, drawing room. And this,' he points at a young man who is standing just inside the door, 'this is Mietek Alexander Szmajke. We call Alex. He come ask marry my sister.'

'Did he marry her?'

'Yes. Good friend. Good brother-in-law.' It's not until some time later that I learn just how good a friend Alex was.

As the lesson progresses, I realise that the times when Dziadek was on leave, while he was at the Officer Academy and right up to the start of the Second World War, were the times he could really relax and enjoy his family home. Before the Academy he'd been in Russia; first at school and then having to assume responsibility for the family. After the war he lived far from home, but in the years he'd illustrated by the space between the pencil and the felt pen, he'd been able to be a carefree, fun-loving young man.

At 'Dzierżkowice', he was surrounded by people of a similar background. As we reach the end of the lesson Dziadek suddenly says, 'Tala come to house for dance.'

'I bet you went for walks in the moonlight together,' I tease. He doesn't answer, just smiles as he closes the photo album.

I discover from his family that circumstances conspired against the relationship between Tala and Dziadek going further. By the time the latter was in a position to ask for Tala's hand in marriage, should he have so wished, he was caught up in fighting and the two didn't meet again until many years later when both of them were already married. The two families, however, were always on friendly terms.

I have been surprised to find that Dziadek has not only a romantic but also a light-hearted side to his nature. He has always seemed such a serious and thoughtful man. Now I learn, again from his family, that there were other occasions when he allowed the lighter side to show.

There's a story about him riding his horse up the wide staircase of the Officers' Mess for a bet. The horse walked up willingly enough, but refused to come down and remained on the landing for some hours – to Dziadek's embarrassment. Finally a vet managed to cajole the poor creature down.

Another story involves him drinking champagne, again with other officers, throwing the glasses into the air and shooting at them as they dropped.

Yet another tale of even more reckless fun is of a game called 'Cuckoo'. This was played in the dark. Everyone hid behind furniture and took it in turns to jump up, call 'Cuckoo' and dive down again. At the call the rest of the players would shoot in the direction of the sound of the voice. Apparently no fatalities or even injuries were reported as a result of these extraordinary activities.

I begin to see Dziadek in a new light.

1928 – August 1939

I thoroughly enjoyed my first posting which was to Suwalki. I became Platoon and later Company Commander there. In fact I remained in the same place for nine years, but my life changed radically when, on 11th November 1937, I was posted to the small town of Kleck. There I joined the Korpus Ochrony Pogranicza or KOP (Border Defence Corps). By then responsibility for border security had passed from police into military hands. My appointment was that of Company Commander of the heavy artillery which was part of a Reserve Battalion. I recruited suitable men from a company stationed in Krakow, then I trained and assessed them. The best were posted to sentry towers along the Polish frontier. The rest trained with the Reserves until suitable postings could be found.

I discovered that none of the other companies had an officer at the helm. Each was commanded by an NCO. The Frontier was in turmoil and regularly strafed by Soviet planes.

'Let's get at them sir,' begged one of my corporals. 'Buggers need a good lesson.'

'It would be a waste of ammunition,' I answered. 'They're flying too high. We'd never hit them.'

The Battalion Commander agreed with me. 'No hope of shooting any of them down,' he said. 'Not only would it be a waste of ammunition but it would be very demoralising for the troops as they'd never be able to achieve a hit.' I asked the NCOs to explain this to the men. It was important that they understood.

At the next meeting with my Commander, I heard disturbing news. 'The Soviets have begun intense infiltration of our territory,' he said. 'While we've been concentrating on air attacks their ground troops were moving forward, almost unnoticed.'

'Perhaps we should carry out training during daylight hours only,' I suggested. 'At night our men could patrol the frontier, set up ambushes and do whatever it takes to repel the Soviets.'

'Excellent,' said the boss. 'Put that into action straight away.'

In spite of our best efforts the situation continued to deteriorate. We were forced to send our more experienced soldiers to help man the frontier posts, replacing them with raw recruits. This movement of men gave the Soviets an excuse to tell the world that 'Poland is mobilising against us.' Their newspapers were full of the story. Western powers, unaware of what was really happening, and unwilling to believe ill of Stalin, chastised the Polish Government.

Life for the people living near the frontier was very tough. Roads were blocked and farms despoiled. Necessities were in short supply. One of my responsibilities, as Company Commander, was to locate and oversee the transport of food and clothing to the children of thirty six schools in my area.

Suddenly the Battalion received a consignment of heavy armaments – Bofors 37mm calibre weapons. As I was the only officer in the whole Regiment with experience of these weapons, I was forced to become Overseeing and Training Commander for the men whose job it would be to use them. This, on top of my other duties.

There were other problems too and, again, I voiced some of my frustrations to my Commanding Officer.

'I had to send all those horses back to the squadrons they came from. They just weren't suitable for the work here.'

'We need horses.'

'I know sir. I've chosen new ones which should arrive tomorrow, but we haven't enough horsemen to ride them yet.' And a couple of days later, 'We've the men and the horses now, sir, *but no ammunition. Also, the cannons came yesterday but we're still waiting for men trained to use them.'*

At this stage, it seemed to me that the fates conspired to make everything as difficult as possible. I unburdened myself to my mother who was staying with me at the time.

'Kostek,' she said 'You know you wouldn't want to be doing anything else.' I could only smile because I knew she was right.

At last, in May 1939, another officer arrived to support me. I had barely briefed him when, in June, I was ordered to Warsaw to participate in an Intelligence Corps Course. The course finished in August and I managed to spend a little time with my mother and two sisters. If I'd known what lay ahead I'd have made more time. I would have tried to get them to safety – but that is with hindsight. On 29th August I left them in my apartment when I was posted to the KOP in Vilno, Lithuania.

Buried Treasure

'This not my spoon.' It was coffee time and Dziadek was holding an inoffensive looking teaspoon up in the air. 'This wrong one.' Then I remembered a story I had heard from Anna some years previously.

When war was declared in 1939, Dziadek was living in a furnished apartment close to the military base in Kleck, a town near the Lithuanian border. He had taken with him a few treasured possessions including a white porcelain mug he's had since childhood, a teaspoon which was exactly the right size for spooning conserve into black Polish tea and an enamel photograph of himself as a baby, a gift from his mother, Maria.

The Enamelled Photograph

Maria was staying with him when he was called away to Border Guard duties so he arranged for his sister, Ania and her daughter, Halinka, to travel to Kleck to be company for Maria.

One evening, as the little household sat at supper, a neighbour hammered at the door.

'The Soviet Army is marching towards Kleck,' he shouted. 'The orders from the Camp Commander are that we should pack a few belongings and be ready to leave by military transport early in the morning. The Soviets will be here within a day or two.'

'Thank God we've a means of getting away. We'll be running for our lives,' declared Maria. 'Ania, you and the child bundle together what you really need and are able to carry. I'll see to my things and pack some food.'

When everything was put ready, Maria had one further task for the family. 'Halinka, you run and fetch a spade from the shed and bring the small oilskin bag which is hanging behind the shed door,' she said. Then she cut some strips of linen from a towel and wrapped each of Dziadek's three treasures separately. She placed them in the oilskin bag and beckoned Ania and Halinka to follow her into the garden. Four paces from the corner of the stone shed she started to dig. With the help of the others she had soon dug a sizeable hole.

'Put these things in carefully, Halinka,' she said, 'and then help me to fill it in.'

By the time the earth had been replaced and the child had thrown some grit and gravel on top and jumped up and down on it, it was impossible to see that the earth had been recently disturbed.

The women spent the evening sewing what money and small jewels they had into the hems of their garments. No one slept much that night and they were all up before dawn, dressed in as many layers of clothing as possible. They had just picked up their bundles and were about to leave the house when they heard a commotion outside. The Russians has arrived early. Tanks were pouring down the main street, people were shouting and in a few moments Soviet soldiers were at the door. Escape was impossible. Within an hour Dziadek's family and countless townspeople were marching to the railway station accompanied by armed guards. There, they were herded into cattle trucks and taken on a nightmare journey to a collective farm in Siberia.

After the war the Soviet Government was not keen to repatriate the people who had been working on farms and in forests and factories in Siberia. They didn't want to lose the cheap labour. Most couldn't afford the train fare home and there were difficulties in locating family members in the West. At last

Dziadek succeeded in discovering the whereabouts of his mother, sister and niece and in 1946 scraped together enough money to enable them to return to Poland. They settled in Gdansk. Letters were exchanged between them regularly via an address in Switzerland.

Because Dziadek had been a member of the Polish Intelligence Corps and had served a prison sentence for 'crimes against the state', he was unable to travel to Poland to visit his family and Maria died in 1956 without seeing her son again. It was not until 1979 that Dziadek managed to save enough money to send for Ania so that she could come to her beloved brother. By that time she was eighty and almost blind. Unable to speak any English she braved the journey alone.

They were too moved to speak when they met. In fact they spent hours just sitting together without any conversation. It was enough just to be together. But Ania had brought an unexpected gift. From the depths of her shabby bag, hidden among the thin and much mended clothes, she withdrew a package and handed it to her brother. He unwrapped it with trembling hands and found his teaspoon, mug and enamel photograph. He gazed at these remnants of a past life unable to find any words. Softly Ania explained.

'A kind friend took me to Kleck last month just after you had sent me the money for my fare. It has changed very much and I didn't really expect to find the things we had buried so long ago. I couldn't believe it when I realised the stone shed was still there on what is now waste ground. My friend dug where I showed him, four paces away from the corner. And there they all were, all the things that we'd buried forty years ago.'

By the time this story had flashed through my mind, I had retrieved the precious teaspoon from the cutlery drawer and Dziadek was happily stirring his coffee before drinking it from his special porcelain mug.

August 1939 – August 1941

Vilno was alive with rumours of war. My first task was to set up a training programme for the troops. At the end of August 1939 a German battleship, 'Schleswig-Holstein', steamed into Gdansk harbour on what was described as a 'diplomatic mission. On 1st September however, its guns began to fire. The war had started. We heard much later how bravely the Westerplatte Garrison at Gdansk and the people of the city fought for six days. At the end there were 300 dead Germans against 15 Polish dead. The Allies declared war on Germany on 3rd September. News of other Nazi attacks and of the Luftwaffe slowly trickled through to us. None of us could sleep.

'The Allies will come to our aid,' we told each other. We kept on training. We continued to repulse many of the Soviet forays over our border. But then, on 17th September the Soviets mounted a full-blown invasion from the east on the pretext of protecting the Ukrainian population. At the same time the Lithuanian Government, siding with the Soviets, decided to incarcerate all members of the Polish Army serving in Lithuania.

'It won't be for long,' we told each other as we tried to make ourselves comfortable in the small cell in Kulatuwa Prison. 'Our army will fight back and, with the help of the Allies, we'll be all right.'

By summer 1940 I had been imprisoned in Wilkowiszki and then Kalwaria. On 10th July, Lithuania, in spite of its loyalty to Soviet Russia, was overrun by the Red Army, and Soviets occupied the country. They took control of the prison and shortly afterwards a guard came to our cell.
'You have five minutes to get your things together.'

'Where are we going?
'Just be ready or there'll be trouble.'

Crammed together in cattle trucks we cheered ourselves up.
'The Allies have promised. They won't fail us.' These words
become our mantra.

The train halted just over the Soviet border. An NKVD[1]*
officer (officer in the Soviet Secret Police) opened the door and,
looking in, shouted, 'Dzierżek? Is KonstantyDzierżek in here?'
  'I am,' I answered.
  'We know all about you. You're a spy.' I was so surprised
that I couldn't answer. He went on, 'We know all about you and
your father working together as spies.' I suddenly realised that
they didn't really know anything. They must have found out that I
had been on an Intelligence Corps course. In their eyes this made
me a spy.
  'You're completely mistaken,' I countered. 'How could I have
spied alongside my father? I was only ten when he died, and
anyway, who do you think we spied for – the Tsar, the Germans?'
The officer was undeterred.
  'We know everything. You're still very young but you're
already a captain. Your promotion has been accelerated because
of your real work. You are a spy and you will be treated
accordingly.'
  Suddenly I lost patience with this blockhead. 'My rank is
immaterial. You look younger than I do yet you are already a
major, although not in the army, it's true, only in the NKVD. Does
that make you a spy?' If he could have reached me he'd have hit
me but we'd been shouting over the heads of fifty or more people.
Then the train jolted into motion. He slammed the door and I
found everyone looking at me.
  A man near me voiced what the rest were thinking. 'You
shouldn't argue with them. It pays to be humble and co-

---

[1]NKVD – Narodnyi komissariat vnutrennikh del (Russian) – translates as Peoples'
Commissariat for Internal Affairs. It was the predecessor of the KGB.

operative.' I turned away, sick at heart. From then until we reached our destination, Kozielsk Prison, I felt that the other occupants of the truck were distancing themselves from me.

Conditions at Kozielsk were not too bad. True, cells were crowded and food scarce and poor, but after the initial inevitable questioning, no-one seemed to take a special interest in me, though my heart sank when I was called to the prison Governor's office one day. He addressed me in Russian. 'I understand you are a fluent Russian speaker.'

I wondered what was coming next. I took a deep breath and answered him in Russian.

'That is true'.

'How does this come about?' I knew I was on shaky ground. I didn't want to say I had been born in Russia because that could be twisted. I might suddenly find myself declared a Russian citizen and be forced to join the Red Army.

'My father was employed to help plan your railways. Our family spent some years in Russia and I was educated there. That's when I learned to speak Russian so fluently.' He seemed satisfied. 'You will now act as interpreter in this prison. Remember that some of my officers are able to speak some Polish so be very careful to make your interpretations accurate.'

On 17th November 1940, I was officially arrested as a spy and charged with committing crimes against the Soviet State. I was moved to the prison in Minsk. On the same day many senior officers were taken out of the prison at Kolzielsk and removed to an unknown place.[2]

The regime at Minsk was much harsher than that of Kolzielsk. As soon as we arrived, guards cut all the buttons from our clothes, including those from trousers and underwear. We weren't even allowed cord or string to keep up our trousers. Guards took

---

[2]Later I learned they were taken to the Katyn forest. There, the Soviets shot and buried more than 4,200 senior Polish Officer. That is the number which was verified by an international committee. If I had not been arrested for spying on that day, I would have been among their number.

my money, watch, silver cigarette case, signet ring – everything I had except for a towel, a piece of soap, a couple of handkerchiefs and a change of underwear. I was given a receipt for my belongings – a worthless piece of paper without a signature.

It was immediately clear that as I was suspected of spying I was to be treated differently from other new arrivals. While they were taken off in groups, presumably to ordinary cells, I was put into a very small cell – a cage really. I couldn't stand upright, I could only squat. The sole light was a very bright naked light bulb above my head.

For no reason at all I started to laugh, perhaps in hysteria, or perhaps because I couldn't allow myself to cry.

The guard opened the door straight away and demanded, 'Why are you laughing?'

In Russian I replied, 'I don't know,' I embellished my answer with a few choice Russian swear words.

'Shut up you idiot!' he shrieked. 'Swearing is forbidden here. Any more of it and you'll finish up in a really happy cell where the food will be first rate.' He ended with a sneering laugh and slammed the door loudly.

I stiffened in the confined space. Each time I was let out to go to the latrine I found it harder to straighten my legs. I received neither food nor water. The bright light and uncomfortable position made it impossible to sleep. The hours crept by. I lost track of time and just when I thought I could bear it no longer, I was hauled out. I had my photograph taken with a number hung round my neck, and my fingerprints recorded. Then I was marched to a general cell.

It was built to house two prisoners. There were twenty two of us crammed inside. There was one bunk bed with no mattress, the tiny window was blocked by a piece of wood and the walls were streaked red and brown with the blood of squashed lice and bugs.

Everyone was sitting on the concrete floor. At last I was given a piece of bread and some water.

I soon learned the system used for interrogation. Usually we were called out in alphabetical order, but sometimes it was random. My first session was carried out by a young NKVD officer who questioned me in Russian. His briefcase lay on the corner of his desk. I immediately noticed some papers sticking out and recognised them as orders which had been sent to me by the KOP battalion in Kleck. I remembered the content of those orders so I knew how to answer the questions.

Throughout all the interrogations I stuck to what I had said to that young officer. Sometimes I was beaten or subjected to other punishments, but I never changed my story. On days when all seemed dark and without hope, I longed for the time the Allies would come to the aid of all loyal Polish people.

On 28ᵗʰ March 1941, without any sort of trial I received my sentence for 'treason against the state.' It was eight years hard labour in an NKVD labour camp 'in a distant place.' The Allies had not come in time to rescue me. I was sent briefly to Kalinos Camp and then, on 28ᵗʰ June, to Colony 35.[3]

On my second day there I was called to the office where I was confronted by an NKVD general. His first question surprised me. 'How did you know there was going to be a German-Soviet war against Poland, Britain, France and their allies? You are a spy, aren't you? That's how you knew.'

I was incredulous. 'Everyone knew,' I said. 'The world's press told us it was going to happen long before war was declared. It was obvious to us all what the Germans were aiming for.'

'So everyone knew about the impending war because of the newspapers?'

---

[3] For information on conditions in the penal colonies/camps and in the prisons and explanation of the cauldron numbers, see the next chapter, entitled 'Transcript of Deposition'.

'Yes. When I was in the KOP, in Stolpcow, the driver of the train from Moscow bought every newspaper from the kiosk on the station. He said he wanted to take them back home with him as news of the coming war didn't figure in the Soviet press.' The general looked uncomfortable for a moment, then said, 'I shall look into this.'

I was called to the office again in the afternoon. 'It appears you told me the truth this morning. I note that you have always stuck exactly to the story you told when you were first questioned. You have never deviated. I know this because I have access to transcripts of all your interrogations.'

'If, as you say, I have always told the truth, then you'll realise that I have done nothing wrong,' I said. 'Why am I being treated as a guilty convict?'

The general would not be drawn. 'All I know is that you are a political prisoner with a sentence of eight years. From today however, even though you must remain in the camp, I will ensure you are given work outside.'

My new task was to collect and place, in piles, planks which were strewn around the camp. They were left from the time of the thaw of last winter's snow. The work was hard. The planks were long and water-logged, but I was unsupervised so I could take my time. I received my food from cauldron 3.

On 15th August I was sent to Colony 33, where I worked on the Siberian Railway. I had no premonition of what lay ahead.

Transcript of Deposition

This document bears witness to the condition in Soviet prisons and labour camps. It is important that the World should not forget.

Conditions in the prison and camps in which I found myself between 17th October 1940 and 16th September 1941.

NKVD Headquarters, Minsk Prison

Before reception into prison all belongings were removed and a receipt was given for some of the items. Everything made from gold was received as 'Yellow Metal' and all silver as 'White Metal'. All metal buttons, hooks and eyes, press studs and buckles were cut from clothes. Occasionally prisoners were permitted to retain a change of underwear, a towel, blanket and a piece of soap to take to their cells. I was not allowed to take tooth powder and toothbrush to mine.

Next, personal details were recorded in an office, where a photograph and fingerprints were taken. This was followed by removal to a cell or detention block.

The cells were filthy, unheated even in winter and with no glass in the small windows. They were sealed with wood or rags. The walls were red with the blood of bugs and lice. In a five man cell, there were twenty-five of us. We slept five to a bed, widthways, in turns. The rest had to sleep on the asphalt floor. There were sometimes a few mattresses filled with sawdust and a few blankets. We were forbidden to sleep during the day.

Our meals consisted of:

Breakfast: 600 grams bread, 'coffee' made from wheat or acorns and, occasionally, 2 sugar cubes.
Midday and evening meals – ¾ litres fish-based soup. Small amounts buckwheat.

Meals were irregular. Sometimes two meals were given out at the same time, often in the middle of the night.

Interrogation of any prisoner always started during the night, once he had settled to sleep, often about 9 pm. He was kept all night until just before reveille at 6 am. He was collected again at 10 am and kept all day. This would continue for 7-12 nights and days without a break. Then he was 'forgotten' for about 15-30 days while others received the same treatment. After that everything would begin again in exactly the same pattern.

Prisoners were searched thoroughly each time they returned to their cells. In order to mortify them, female prisoners were strip-searched and left naked. In some cells males and females were incarcerated together. During the days and nights of interrogation it was forbidden to talk to or even look at anyone outside your own cell.

Commonly prisoners were beaten with rubber hoses, rulers, sticks – anything that came to hand. Some were subjected to electric shocks, to having burning objects pushed between their fingers and pins inserted under fingernails. They had turpentine poured up their nostrils, were kicked in the shins and had stools, on which they were sitting, kicked from under them. Personally, I was forced to stand on tiptoes in a tight and narrow cell for several hours under a 'whirlwind' or jet of very hot air. Women prisoners were usually stripped naked before being subjected to the same treatment.

Prisoners were entitled to 15 minutes a week in the 30 metre square exercise yard. In reality, we were allowed only between 5 and 10 minutes about twice a month.

After sentencing, while waiting for transportation, prisoners were put in holding cells designed for 20 people. Between 150 and 240 people were crammed in. In cells, 6, 7 and 95 there was not even space to sit down. In some cells prisoners were forced to sit naked on cement floors. The punishment cells were very cramped with no light. Occupants received 450 grams of bread, water and, on every fifth day, some soup.

The guards were vicious. Talking was forbidden. Twice a day all prisoners from a cell were taken to filthy lavatories meant for four people. There was never time to take advantage of the amenity properly. The male guards often climbed over the partitions of women's lavatories and wash rooms.

There was no real medical care. Sick prisoners were viewed through a grille in the door. Unconscious ones were removed to hospital where they were tended by untrained nurses.

Forced Labour Camps

Barracks in the camps comprised either mud huts or buildings constructed of tree trunks of 5-7 cm diameter. Bunks were made of the same type of tree trunks with no mattresses. Floors, too, were of tree trunks which were laid over water.

Inmates worked for thirteen hours a day excluding travel time, which could be up to two hours each way. My work at one camp was moving barrow loads of wet clay. The 'norm' or expected average amount to be moved was 7.20 cubic metres daily.

Prisoners were fed according to the norm, from cauldrons 1, 2, 3, 7 and 10. I give below examples of the amount of food given to prisoners achieving the highest and lowest norms. The latter were usually sick, old or weak.

105% of norm Cauldron 3
1000 grams bread daily
Breakfast – ¾ litre wheat 'coffee', 5 grams cooked meat or 20 grams fish
Midday and evening meals – ¾ litres soup made from meat stock

Below 75% of norm Cauldron 1
550 grams bread daily
All meals – hot water

The cost of food was deducted from prisoners' wages.

Medical care was provided by lepkom (trusted prisoners) with no medical training or experience. No medication was available. To register as sick, a prisoner must have visible wounds or a temperature of above 38 degrees. Unconscious or seriously wounded prisoners were removed to the hospital. There, I believe, conditions were acceptable. Some care was provided by prisoners who were qualified doctors. Most of these were Polish.

Any infringement of rules resulted in punishment. This comprised standing outside naked for several hours where one was prey to vicious mosquitoes and midges or to exposure to bitter cold and frostbite.

Work was done in the ragged remains of a prisoner's own clothes. No clothes of any kind were supplied at any of the forced labour camps in which I was incarcerated.

I testify to the truth of this deposition
KonstantyDzierżek
Captain
Date: 29th June 1942

September 1941

News of an amnesty for Polish prisoners was slow to reach us in the forced labour camps. The Soviets were in no hurry to enlighten us. They realised that once we heard the glad tidings we would no longer be their slaves. At last, in late September 1941, the news leaked out and I stood staring through the high wire fence trying to take in the fact that, theoretically at any rate, I was a free man.

I sought an interview with the Commandant. Looking at my documents he realised I was a captain. He saluted and invited me to sit down. Times had certainly changed.

'Ask your people to be ready to move. You will be taken by road to the Kalinos Camp and from there those who so wish can travel to join the army.'

At Kalinos, where I had been incarcerated from March until the end of April, the difference in atmosphere was immediately noticeable.

'Look,' I said to my friend Olek who was standing next to me, 'there are still guards on the towers but what's happened to their big guns?' We strolled to the edge of our zone and chatted to people in the next one. The camp held about ten thousand. It was divided by barbed wire into zones. From the air it must have looked a bit like a chess board. We had never been allowed to go anywhere near the zone next to us. When we were five paces away a guard would shout at us and if we took no notice a beating ensued. Now we were allowed to exchange news and views and even share cigarettes and food with our neighbours.

'The food's better isn't it?' Olek remarked.

'Well, the bread's poor and the soup's thin but there's more of it I suppose,' I replied.

'Someone overheard two guards talking. They said that we're all going to be getting our exit papers over the next few days.' chimed in a man who was nearby. 'They're going to distribute them alphabetically.'

'And,' added Olek, 'one of the women who cleans the offices, told me she'd overheard that the Polish Army is assembling in Buzuluk.'

At last the day came when it was the turn of those of us whose surnames began with 'D' to receive our papers but no-one came for me. No-one came for me the next day either. Then the 'E' people were called and I started to feel very worried. 'Shall I try to see the Commandant?' I asked myself. Just then I noticed one of the guards picking up cigarette ends, other bits of rubbish and even stones. He was swearing under his breath and glanced angrily in my direction. Something was afoot, I knew. Perhaps an important visitor was due. If so, I'll approach him with my concerns, I decided. He'll probably carry more weight than the Commandant. I picked up a few stones and put them into the rubbish sack. 'What's this about?' I asked casually.

'Bloody bigwigs – always make extra work.' I deposited some more rubbish into his sack.

'Bigwigs? Who's coming?'

'A procurator from Moscow, this morning sometime. The bosses are all shaking in their shoes, everything has to be perfect and guess who has to do all the work?'

'A magistrate? Great!' I thought, and drifted away from the guard to take up a position by the wire from where I could see the administrative offices.

An hour later I saw a well-dressed gentleman walking to the office. He was looking around, apparently assessing his surroundings. He stopped near the buildings as if waiting for someone. I thought he might be the procurator. I made for the gate but was stopped by a guard.

'No moving between zones.' He snapped. 'Things may have got lax but they're not that lax.' At that moment six ragged prisoners arrived at the gate. They were carrying a long pole from which hung six buckets. They were on the way to the kitchens to collect soup for their hut. Six more people followed them. They would collect the bread. While the guard's attention was diverted by this procession I attached myself to the group of bread carriers. I put my head down and passed through the gate, unnoticed.

As soon as it was safe I left them and went up to the man I thought must be the procurator.

'Excuse me sir.' I addressed him in Russian and he turned to me in surprise.

'I wonder if you can help me.' I introduced myself and explained what had happened. I finished by saying, 'You're an important man, sir. You could ask what has happened to my papers if you wished... if you were willing to help me.'

'What's the hurry? You'll get out soon enough and at least you have food and shelter here.'

I felt anger rising. I wanted to ask whether he would want to remain in prison one day longer than necessary but I bit back a sharp reply. 'I have heard that the Polish Army is assembling in Buzuluk, sir. I am very anxious to join it as soon as possible and take part in the battle against the Nazis, our common enemy.'

The procurator nodded his head in approval. I saw I had won him over. 'I'll enquire on your behalf,' he said. Then he bowed, I saluted and he walked away into the office of the Chief of the NKVD. Feeling triumphant I stood outside the kitchen until the string of food carriers emerged. They were surprised when I offered to help. Thus, again unnoticed, I slipped back into my own zone.

A few minutes later a soldier ran into the zone shouting, 'Dzierżek! Dzierżek!'

'Yes? I'm here.' I shouted back. 'What do you want?' He hurried over to me.

'You must come at once. The NKVD Chief wants you. Come quickly.'

Suddenly I felt sure that the procurator had done what I had asked of him, so I said firmly, 'I'll collect my sack from the hut first.' The soldier became agitated, clearly scared he'd be in trouble if we delayed. I walked with measured tread and retrieved my small bundle of belongings. For some reason, I couldn't define, I felt that power was shifting slightly in my direction. Until now prisoners had been marched everywhere but I chose to walk out of my zone in spite of the soldier's obvious wish to hurry. We arrived at the Chief's office. The soldier knocked and indicated that I should enter. I did so. I placed my bundle on the floor by the door and stood still.

The Chief was sitting behind a big desk. He beckoned me over and indicated that I should sit down. 'Having looked through your papers,' he said, 'I see you were born in Rżew in Central Russia.'

I could see how his mind was working. The threat of conscription to the Red Army loomed once more. 'That is correct, but you'll know that at the time I was born Poland didn't appear on a map of the world at all. It had been stolen by bandits – by Germans, Austrians and by the Tsarina Catherine. My parents resided in one of the places stolen by Catherine so even if I'd been born there I would still have been born "in Russia". As an educated man, you'll know that.' He looked uncomfortable. He knew that I knew he was not an educated man. I went on, 'It so happens that I was born in Rżew but my parents were Polish and I am Polish to the core. My father was employed by the Russian Government to help plan the railway. That's why the family moved to Rżew.'

There was a long silence. Then the Chief said, 'How did Comrade Procurator General come to know you?'

'Procurator **General?**' I said to myself. I hadn't realised that the man I'd spoken to about my papers was the top magistrate in the country. Suddenly I remembered some words of my father's.

'Bluff, my boy,' he'd said to me. 'Always look as if you know what you're doing and you can bluff your way out of almost any *situation.' I stood up so that I could look down on the Chief and I spoke icily.*

'If the Procurator General has not seen fit to explain our relationship then I don't feel it's my place to do so. By all means go and ask him how he knows me. I'll come with you if you like.' I started to walk towards the door. Clearly aghast, the Chief leapt to his feet.

'No, no, there is no need for that, no need at all. I asked you only out of politeness.' I turned to see him scribble across my documents 'Lived in Poland.' He handed them to me with a chit giving me permission to leave the camp at any time.

I held the documents tightly in my hand. Now I was assured of my release I thought I could push the Chief further. I drew myself up to my full six feet two inches. My clothes might be ragged but I had not forgotten how to stand like an Officer. 'How am I to live between now and arriving at Buzuluk?' I asked. 'Here is the receipt for articles confiscated when I entered Minsk Prison. Have they arrived here so that I may collect them?' The Chief shook his head and opened his mouth to answer but I went on, 'I have no food and no money but I do have this receipt also given to me at Minsk. It shows what I am owed for my work there. Will you exchange it for cash?'

'I regret that it is not in my remit to do so but...'

I broke in, 'Am I to starve then?'

'No, no, of course not.' His tone was conciliatory. 'Here's a chit you can use at the NKVD shop. You can get food supplies from there. Here is one for the Reclamation Office. Go there and reclaim your belongings. Also, as a special privilege and because of your relationship with the Procurator General, here is a chit to take to the Kit Store.' He glanced down at my boots, which had several holes in them, and took in my thin, ragged trousers and coat. 'You will be issued with new kit.' He handed over a final signed piece of paper and I realised I had got all I could out of him. I'd done better than I'd expected. I thanked him, picked up my bundle and left.

The disagreeable man behind the counter in the Reclamation Office didn't bother to look up when I entered. He simply grunted. Angrily I threw the chit on the counter under his nose so that he saw the Chief's signature. His manner changed immediately. 'I'll find your belongings without delay.' I followed him to a large room in which the pathetic confiscated bundles were stacked untidily. He looked about him and located the place where my things should be.

'I'm sorry, they don't seem to be here,' he said nervously.

'Why is this place in such a mess?' I demanded. 'It's no wonder you can't find anything.'

'Don't be angry. It's really difficult to keep up with all the comings and goings, I'm sorry.' He consulted a list and decided that my belongings hadn't yet arrived from Minsk. He became helpful. 'I suggest you take this chit, which I'll make out in your name, to the office next door and you can make an official complaint. They'll arrange for Minsk to send your stuff over. It will only take between five and seven days.'

'Thank you but forget it,' I said. I certainly wasn't going to hang around there for another week or so. It wasn't worth it for just a few things which had probably been stolen anyway.

I had more success at the NKVD shop. The officer there noticed the Chief's signature straight away and treated me with respect. He handed over three loaves of good bread, 750 grams of sugar cubes, a packet of real tea, 2 kilograms of fatty salt bacon, four packets of buckwheat, four jars of pork and beans, a large piece of Russian sausage and even 100 top quality Soviet cigarettes. I was amazed and delighted but simply thanked him and accepted it all as my due.

My last call at the Kit Store proved just as satisfactory. I was given new shoes, a pair of trousers, a fufajka (padded jacket) and a field cap. The good thing was that they were all Soviet issue. Instinctively I knew that this, along with my fluent Russian, would be very useful over the coming months. I stood still outside the store for a moment. I felt triumphant, but I knew I was at the beginning of a new set of challenges. The Soviets would not make it easy for me, or anyone else, to reach the Polish Army. However, I had an advantage. I knew the Soviet psyche well. I knew that everyone, from the lowliest peasant to the highest official, lived in fear. Fear of being accused of inefficiency, of not being wholeheartedly committed to The Cause and, worst of all, fear of being accused of sabotage, the penalty for which was death. My latest experiences brought home to me, afresh, the necessity of demanding what I wanted in a hectoring, almost bullying way. That alone would get results in this Soviet age. If I simply asked, I would get nothing and if I begged all would be lost. Thus, mentally ready, and with food and decent clothes, I felt it was time to enquire at the local station about a train to carry me in the direction of Buzuluk.

It was an incredible feeling to walk out through the gates of the camp, waving my pass at the guards. I felt light headed with freedom and hardly noticed the weight of my bundle. Other freed prisoners were walking alongside me to the station, but later I couldn't recall the faces of any of them.

I was astonished to find several hundred Polish people waiting at the station. 'No trains running,' one of them informed me. 'Not for us, anyway.' I saw several empty wagons and an engine in a siding and went to find the stationmaster. He was surprised to see a 'Soviet officer' and became nervous.

'What's going on?' I demanded. 'Why are you cluttering the station with these people? Load them on to those trucks and send them on their way towards Buzuluk.'

'The trucks and engine brought supplies here, from Kotlatz, for repairs and extensions to the railway track,' the man stammered. 'They're not due back there until later today.'

'Is there a train due from Kotlatz?' I snapped.

'No sir, the next one is not until tomorrow morning.'

'Do you usually carry passengers in those trucks when you send them back to Kotlatz?'

'No sir, they always go back empty ready for more supplies of wood and metal.'

'That is gross inefficiency,' I bellowed. 'If you don't get those trucks and that engine ready within the next hour to carry these people to Kotlatz, I will report your behaviour to your seniors. Do you understand?' He did understand – and within an hour I, and about three hundred others, were on our way to Kotlatz.

September 1941 continued

'Get into an orderly queue!' were the first words I heard, bellowed across the milling crowds as our train drew into Kotlatz. The chaos was appalling. It seemed to me that thousands of people were queuing – for tickets, for water, for the lavatory. Others wandered about, unsure what to do. I realised that 'my people' as I had come to think of those on the train, would soon become lost in the multitude so I sent messengers to all the carriages instructing everyone to meet me in the gardens just outside the station.

It took half an hour for us all to assemble. I stood on a broken bench and shouted to make myself heard. 'Thank you for coming here as I asked,' I started, hoping I sounded more confident than I felt. 'I am now going to fetch food for everyone. It is important that you wait here for my return. If you leave you will so easily get lost and then I won't be able to help you.' There were nods and murmurs of assent so I set off through steady drizzle to the NKVD office near the station.

'I am a Polish officer,' I told the official. 'I have brought three hundred people who have been released from Kalinos Camp. We're on our way to Buzuluk, where the Polish Army is assembled. All of the men and many women wish to join that army in order to fight against our common enemy, the Nazis. Some of my people haven't eaten for two days. I require food for them.'

'I can't give you food retrospectively I'm afraid,' he said. At least he hadn't said an outright "No".

'That's a pity but it's understandable,' I answered. 'However, as we are to make a long journey, will you give us provisions for the next few days?' I think he must have been impressed by my

uniform and with my apparent authority, for he agreed and I left with a lorry load of food.

Back in the gardens, I chose some helpers to distribute rations. By now it was dark and no easy task. I knew there would be no more trains leaving Kolatz that night so, when all the people had eaten, I told them to make themselves as comfortable as they could in the station reception area or, when space ran out, in the open air, and I settled myself down for a few hours' sleep.

Early the next morning I picked my way across the sleeping crowds on the station concourse. First, I took stock of what stood in the sidings. There were many dirty and neglected cattle trucks and a Pullman carriage divided into First and Second Classes. Feeling grateful for my experience on the railways, I noted the numbers of the best trucks. Then I presented myself at the Stationmaster's office. The door was ajar. I pushed it open and stepped inside. A slovenly individual looked up from the newspaper he was reading.

'I've come here to give you a chance to redeem yourself,' I thundered. 'I have never seen such incompetence as I have found on your station. I'm working closely with the NKVD. In fact they are supplying food for the people I've brought here en route to Buzuluk.' By now the man was on his feet, clearly very frightened. 'I've found sabotage on all sides here. The rolling stock is neglected, the station is not properly supervised and you see fit to sit here reading the paper when there is mayhem outside…need I go on?'

'No sir, please stop. How can I redeem myself? Just say what you want and if it's in my power I'll give it to you.' I passed him the scrap of paper on which I'd written the numbers of the trucks.

'I want these trucks, cleaned to the highest standard, along with the Pullman carriage. I want an engine with engineers to drive and service it, and I want a train timetable so that I can work out when would be the best time for us to leave.'

'Yes sir. I'll do everything you ask.' He produced a timetable and I saw that it would be best for us to leave early on the morrow.

'Do whatever is necessary to register this train as military transport,' I instructed. 'I shall return with my people before nightfall. We'll spend the night on the train and then, first thing tomorrow, we'll be on our way. Is that clear?'

'Yes sir. Thank you.' The sun was shining as I walked back to pass on the good news to my people. The dazzling sunlight just suited my mood.

'I am a captain in the Polish Army, sir. My name is May. I gather that you are Captain Dzierżek and in charge of this transport. Can I be of any assistance to you?' A pleasant-faced man was suddenly at my side. I was in the midst of supervising the passengers as they boarded the newly cleaned train.

'I would be most grateful for your help, Captain. If you can find some paper, please will you visit each wagon? Make a list of everyone inside and appoint a starosta (supervisor to maintain discipline) and organise distribution of food and water.' Captain May produced a small notebook and pencil stub from his pocket and set to work immediately.

When everybody was on board I enlisted some volunteers to unload provisions from the lorry and stack them in the third class and in one section of the second class compartments of the Pullman carriage. I reserved one compartment for Captain May and myself. We had a toilet and wash basin. Hot water could be obtained from the engine. I reserved another compartment as a sick bay in case anyone should become seriously ill. I felt guilty because the other passengers would have to make do with buckets of hot water and the holes in the floors of wagons. I knew however, that if I were to remain in charge of what Captain May now told me were two thousand three hundred refugees I must hold myself apart.

Late that night, after the evening meal had been distributed, Captain May and I talked over plans. We agreed that I should be responsible for obtaining food as his Russian wasn't very good. He would help with organisation and discipline but, even though we were of equal rank, he insisted I should be in overall command. 'You have much more experience of Soviet Russia than I have,' he said. 'You understand how everything works.' I saw the sense in his argument and agreed.

I had a sudden idea and went to see the stationmaster once more. At first he was alarmed at my reappearance but I thanked him for his co-operation. 'You have shown that you can be efficient and helpful,' I said. 'You have furthered the war effort by your prompt attention to my requests.' The man beamed at me.

'I'm grateful you think so, Captain. If there's anything more I can do...'

'There is one thing more. I need to send a telegram to the next station so that I can order food ahead. Without demur, he handed me a telegraph form. Thus, free and quite illegally, I was able to ensure food for that evening for everyone on the train. It was the first of many such telegrams I was to send.

Early next morning I visited the engineers. I gave them salt fish, some sugar and dried fruit from which they could make tchay (fruit tea). They were delighted and promised to do their best to ensure that the journey was trouble-free. Within a few minutes we were on our way.

The telegram system for ordering food worked well for a couple of days. Then we arrived at a station where no food was available. Captain May told the starostas to organise the cleaning of the wagons and then to allow everyone off the train for exercise and to use the paltry toilet facilities.

Meanwhile, boosted by my last success, I walked into the stationmaster's office. A man leapt up angrily, 'What do you think you're doing, Pig Face?' he roared. 'Can't you read the notice on the door? It says MEMBERS OF THE PUBLIC ARE FORBIDDEN TO ENTER.'

I replied in a soft voice. 'Be quiet and listen to me. I'm not a member of the public, I'm a member of the army – a captain. I *don't want your opinion. You can speak when you're spoken to. What I need is a railway map, a telegraph form and the food I ordered ahead. That is, food for two thousand three hundred people.' The man was silent, sullen for a moment, as if considering the legitimacy of my authority, and then he pushed the railway map towards me. I swept a few things off his desk in order to spread it out. I looked at the timetable alongside the map, making a few notes. Then I looked up. My words and tone were having the desired effect on him. He was uneasy. 'The food must be ready by 1400 hours. He nodded and went out to organise it. A clerk appeared and I repeated my request for a telegraph form.*

'We don't have any forms for private citizens.'

'Did I ask for a form for a private citizen?' I retorted, standing up straight and looking as authoritative as I knew how to. 'This is military business.' He produced the form and I left him sending my message. I slammed the door very loudly on the way out to demonstrate that I was someone of importance. The food was ready at the appointed time. Volunteers loaded it into the train and we were once more on our way.

Several days later we arrived at a station at which food should have been ready for us, in line with orders given by telegram. The station was deserted except for a porter and a workman. 'Where's the mess?' I asked the former. He pointed behind the station buildings. I walked in the direction indicated and found a row of army huts. In front of one was a small table on which there were a few slices of bread and a little meat. I was gazing in disbelief at this 'spread' when a man approached.

'I'm the Mess Manager,' he said. 'This food is for you.'

'I've got two thousand three hundred people on my military transport,' I shouted. 'How far do you think this will go? I telegraphed ahead so that you would be ready for us.'

The man was dumbfounded for a moment, then stammered, 'I...I'm sorry sir, there's been a misunderstanding. If you'll be patient my workers will supply soup and bread for your transport.' He ran off to organise the food and I followed him into one of the huts to ensure he did as he promised. I left him shouting orders at a group of women and then I walked back to the platform. I couldn't believe my eyes. The track was empty. My train had disappeared.

September– October 1941

'Where's the train gone?' I shrieked at a workman, the only person on the platform.

'Left a few minutes ago,' he called back. He walked over to me. 'The stationmaster ordered us to send it on its way. We're expecting a train, one that's a day late. It's full of civilian refugees.'

I knew I had to act fast if I wanted to rejoin my train. I wasn't sure which official I should speak to so I decided to try summoning them all. 'Get the local military commander, the NKVD chief and the stationmaster immediately.' I ordered.

The military commander whose office was next to the NVKD headquarter arrived first. 'What's all the fuss about?' he demanded.

'Sabotage,' I replied. 'A military transport has been sent away without food and without me, the Commanding Officer.'

'It's not my fault,' he answered quickly. 'I was occupied checking there was enough food for your transport. Your train was early so we weren't prepared for you.'

I let that pass and turned to the NKVD commander who had just joined us. 'I apologise that there was no-one here to greet you and to find out your plans,' he blustered. 'I was sure your train would be late – they always are.'

By now the stationmaster had arrived. He started to make excuses. 'I was very busy when I heard the news of the delayed refugee train. I didn't have time to come and tell you I'd decided to move your train on. I instructed a porter to inform you.'

I was silent for a moment and let my eyes sweep scornfully over these incompetent men. Then I said slowly, 'The fact remains *that my transport has been moved without my permission and that the two thousand three hundred people on board will go hungry. Furthermore, the food for those people, which at this very moment is being prepared in the mess, will be wasted. All that can certainly be described as sabotage. Don't you agree?' More explanations and excuses followed, during which I was thinking quickly. I interrupted. 'I won't report this appalling oversight to higher authorities if you do four things. First, phone the next station and ask the stationmaster to stop my train there. Secondly, as my people will miss the soup and bread being made ready for them here, you must supply dry provisions instead. Thirdly, you must take me and those dry provisions to my train as soon as possible. Finally, you must use the hot food which is being prepared here to feed the civilian refugees you are expecting.'*

The stationmaster looked unhappy. 'I would very much like to help you sir,' he said in a conciliatory tone, 'but alas I have no engine here to transport you and the provisions to the next station.' Once more my knowledge of railways came to my aid.

'I noticed there was an engine at the last station we passed through – only a few miles back. Order it to be sent here. It can push the trucks, carrying me and the provisions to the next station where they can be unloaded on to my train. Then the engine can bring the empty trucks back here to the sidings. This will leave the track clear for the civilian train to stop. Do you know where that train is at the moment?'

'It's two stations back, waiting for me to phone through with clearance.'

'Then do as I say as fast as you can. By the time the food in the mess is cooked the civilians will be here to eat it. If all goes smoothly I will make sure that those in authority hear about it.' The stationmaster looked helplessly at the NKVD commander who gave a little nod. The military man shrugged but agreed. At once, everything was set in motion.

Within an hour the dry food was being unloaded from the wagons into our own food store in the third class compartment. We had so much food now that it was a tight squeeze.

'All to the good,' commented Captain May. 'People join us at every station. We're up to about two thousand seven hundred now.'

'And we don't know what the future holds,' I added.

Our most memorable stop was at Tashkent. We were greeted by the NKVD and military commanders and a string orchestra. I was led to the large dining hut. In front of it was a table on which small amounts of the 'dishes of the day' were arrayed alongside a complaints book. The duty officer and a doctor were tasting each dish in turn and I was invited to do the same. Meat stew, vegetables and even a sweet pudding were lined up. I wrote in the book, 'Delicious – well-cooked and tasty', and after a full meal, I added, 'Generous portions.' I congratulated the commander of the field kitchen and he beamed with pleasure. It took some hours for all my people to eat and the orchestra played beautifully the whole time. They were still playing as our train pulled away from Tashkent station.

At Orenburg I received orders from Polish Command that we should not go to Buzuluk but to Samarkand, where the army was now assembling.

'It's not going to be easy to reschedule your transport,' grumbled the stationmaster.

'But it has to be done,' I countered. 'Remember we are on the same side, fighting the Nazis.'

At Samarkand we heard that our army was now in Farab, a river port on the Amu Dar'ya River. Would we ever catch up with it? I kept my feelings to myself.

'Nearly there,' I said to Captain May. ' Soon we can hand our precious cargo over to the authorities and work towards actually taking part in this war again.' I was depressed because a number of people including women and children had died over the past few days. In spite of our current, adequate supply of food and water some had been too weak and malnourished to survive the journey. All we'd been able to do for them and their families was to bury the bodies, with due reverence, at the side of the railway track. I felt each death as a personal failure. I had said I'd bring them to safety and I hadn't been able to keep my promise.

On 8th October, as our train drew into Farab, a young NKVD officer sprinted along the platform to my compartment. 'I need the Commanding Officer,' he shouted. I jumped down and presented myself. To my surprise, he said breathlessly, 'Barges are ready to take you to Nukus. Order your people to disembark in groups. Each group must be marched to the quay and then they must board the barges. There is no time to be lost.'

I knew that Nukus was about five hundred kilometres down river. I also knew that some of my people would not to survive a river journey without time to rest. 'Where are my orders from the Polish Authorities?' I demanded. He looked dismayed.

'I don't know. I'm simply delivering a message as I was told to do. My Chief is in his office which is in the port buildings.'

'I'll speak to him there.' I turned to Captain May. 'Please order disembarkation. Tell the starostas to take their people in an orderly fashion, and to assemble them close to the port buildings.' The young officer was disconcerted, but I ignored this and asked him to take me to the office.

The Chief was furious. 'How dare you question my orders?' he stormed.

'Because you aren't the person I take orders from,' I answered quietly. 'Show me the orders from my superior and I will make sure that all my people are on the barges within an hour.'

His face turned red with anger as he spluttered, 'I haven't got orders for you from your bloody superior officer. All I know is that I must send you to Nukus. Those are my orders from my superior officer.'

'I'm sorry but I can't accept orders from the NKVD. We'll wait here until the order comes to me from Polish Command. You must allow me to send a telegram to the Polish Authorities. I'm sure they will reply as soon as possible.'

He saw there was nothing he could say to change my mind, but he had a trick up his sleeve. 'Damn your impudence! You needn't think I'm going to feed you and your rabble while you wait here. You can starve to death for all I care.' In my mind's eye I saw the provisions we still had on our train. We might have to ration supplies but we wouldn't starve. He looked disappointed when I didn't react to his threat and with bad grace he allowed me to send the telegram.

'As we might be here for a few days,' I said. 'We'll need to dig latrines. Where shall we place them?'

'Nowhere!' He saw another opportunity to repay me for my insolence. 'No food and no latrines.'

'In that case,' I countered 'We'll have to use the square just outside this office. It will be most convenient.'

He knew he was beaten and shouted to the young officer to bring spades and to show me where the latrines could be dug. He had one more nasty surprise for me. 'You have been very uncooperative. I will not accommodate your riff raff under cover. You will all have to manage outside.'

On 16th October the order came from the Polish Authorities that I should take as many people as I could with me to Nukus, leaving the rest to follow as soon as possible. I was instructed to stay in Nukus until I received further communication. Nothing was mentioned about joining up with the army and I was very disappointed but set about following the order I'd been given. I managed to obtain food for all the travellers and decided to take Captain May, my friend, Lieutenant Jagielski, and an Aide to act as my assistants. Five barges towed by a tugboat left Farab. As it was almost dusk we didn't get far. It was dangerous to travel on the river at night because of strong currents and sand bars. The barges were crammed with people. Conditions on board were terrible. The decks ran with filthy water and there was very little *room to sit or even stand. At night we camped on the banks and lit fires to cook our food and keep the tigers at bay.*

During stops Captain May and I visited the other barges. I developed terrible ulcers on one foot and found it difficult to walk. They were so painful that I removed my shoe and then couldn't get it back on. The ulcers began to spread up my leg. After four days we reached the Port of Nukus and disembarked. I was unable to muster everyone and seek accommodation because I was virtually immobile. I sent Jagielski to find Captain May to ask him to take control, only to discover that he and my Aide had decided to walk the three kilometres into the town of Nukus, followed by several hundred of our people.

I felt helpless, but with Jagielski's help I struggled ashore. He left me propped against a wall but returned in a few minutes. 'I've found shelter for us. It's not far,' he said.

'Sorry,' I apologised as I leaned heavily on him. We struggled to a small shed next to a derelict cinema. It was pitch black inside so we left the door open. I could do nothing but sink to the floor.

'Your leg is dreadful,' Jagielski said after taking a quick look. 'We'll have to do something about it.'

'Would you ask amongst our people if anyone has iodine or peroxide, please?' I replied. 'Anything that will stop the infection spreading.'

Half an hour elapsed. I lay still in the dark, trying to concentrate on something other than the painful throbbing of my leg. Then there was a knock at the door and a shape appeared in the doorway.

'Captain Dzierżek?'

'Yes.'

A man came over and bent down to shake my hand. 'I am Falski. I used to practice medicine in Lvov. I hear you have a bad leg. Will you allow me to examine it?'

'Thank you, yes.'

He opened the door wide and asked me to shuffle as close to it as I could. He spent a long time examining my leg, feeling it and even sniffing it. Finally he straightened up and said, 'It's not good but it could be worse. It certainly needs immediate attention. Have you any money?'

The man seemed genuine, but I couldn't be sure. He might not be a doctor at all. He could be a rogue looking for a chance to rob me so I answered, 'None at all, I'm afraid.'

'Nor have I. Have you anything you could exchange?'

'I have nothing except the clothes I'm wearing and this shoe which I can't get on.'

'I'm in exactly the same position,' said the doctor. 'Still, I'm sure I'll find something to help. Someone told me there used to be a pharmacy near here. It's been ransacked I believe, but I might find something. I'll go and see.' Before I could say anything else he hurried away. I wondered if I would see him again.

Almost immediately, Jagielski returned. 'No-one has any medical supplies left at all I'm afraid,' he said regretfully. 'But I managed to borrow this little bucket and bowl. There's a chai chana (tea house) just round the corner. I'll ask them for some hot water so that we can wash your leg'

He was back within five minutes, and while I washed my leg I told him about Dr Falski. Then I tore the sleeves from my only clean shirt, made a rough bandage and Jagielski helped me to wrap it around the worst affected area.

We had just finished when the doctor walked through the door, beaming. 'Look what I've got,' he cried triumphantly. He was holding a huge apothecary's display bottle, full of yellow liquid. 'It's disinfectant. If it hasn't deteriorated it will cure your leg. It should be all right. This glass stopper will have kept the air out. I've no idea what's in it, that's a Soviet secret, but I do know that it is extremely effective.'

'How will you know if it's all right?' I asked.

'Easy,' he replied. He removed the stopper, dipped his finger in and put his finger in his mouth. He pulled a face but then smiled. 'It's fine.' I tried not to wince when the disinfectant was applied. He re-bandaged the leg and said he would return the *next day. I thanked him warmly. I was now convinced he was genuine.*

I spent a restless and uncomfortable night, but thought the leg hurt a little less by morning – or was it my imagination?

Dr Falski arrived early. He followed the same procedure for examining me as he had the day before. 'Do you know,' he exclaimed excitedly, 'It's no worse, therefore it must be better!' He applied more disinfectant. 'Walk as little as possible and I'll be back this evening.'

Later Jagielski went out for a while and I lay in the dark trying to work out a plan to avoid going to a collective farm. I had a sudden idea – if I could just get the NVKD on my side. I realised that most of my people would have to go to farms unless I had new orders soon. Working on a farm was a means of obtaining food and shelter. It would be necessary to make a list of names and which areas everyone went to so that they could all be contacted when the time came for us to shake Soviet soil from our shoes and join up with the army. I worried at the subject all day but cheered up considerably when the doctor arrived and found the swelling on my leg almost gone. That night I slept well.

The next morning Dr Falski arrived with two empty bottles, an old car tyre and some string. Before he explained what these were for he looked at my leg. 'It's back to normal!' he cried. 'Well, almost normal.' He laughed at the look on my face, for my leg had turned a vivid yellow, presumably as a result of the disinfectant. 'Never mind the colour. That will fade. The fantastic thing is that we have saved your leg!'

'You have saved my leg,' I corrected him, 'and I can never thank you sufficiently.'

He brushed this aside and handed Jagielski one bottle and me the other. 'Hold these still while I fill them from the big bottle,' he instructed. 'You can have one and I'll take the other. I'll take the residue in the apothecary's bottle back to the pharmacist as I promised.' That accomplished, he got out his knife and cut a piece off the tyre. 'I'll make a sandal for you to wear as your foot is still rather sore and it would be best not to force it into your shoe. He made holes in the strip of rubber, tried it against my foot, nodded and threaded string through the holes. 'Try it on,' he said.

'It's a perfect fit,' I exclaimed.

Jagielski put a handful of buckwheat from our supplies into a little bag and gave it to the doctor. 'It's not much,' I said. 'Nothing would be enough,'

Dr Falski seemed moved by our gift and walked to the door saying, 'Captain, you are cured. That is enough for me but I do thank you for your generosity,' and then he was gone.

October 1941

'Polish prostitutes? Are you sure?'

'Yes, from Lvov.' Jagielski spoke with certainty. 'I overheard two NKVD officers talking about them. My Russian's not very good but I'm sure I've got it right. They called them "happy ladies" and the NKVD is going to force them to work on collective farms as slaves. They've got them holed up on the other side of the river.'

It was the day after the doctor had pronounced my leg cured and I was managing to get around on one shoe and the tyre sandal. I'd just visited many of the people who had travelled on my transport. They were camping in various old buildings and still living off the dry provisions we had brought with us. I'd need to see the NKVD commander and arrange for food to be provided and also discuss their going to collective farms in the surrounding countryside but first I must attend to the prostitutes. I'd realised, as soon as Jagielski told me what he'd heard, that their future was likely to be very grim unless I could intervene.

I managed to find a boat to take me over the Amu-Dar'ya and, as I approached the buildings near the quay, I heard a babble of women's voices. I stood still for a moment as I glimpsed a couple of scantily clad girls. It appeared that they were just getting up.

A pretty, smartly dressed young woman came out of one of the buildings and walked over to me. 'Can I help you?' she asked, glancing down at my 'sandal'. 'I am the brigadier (person in charge) of the women housed here. What can I do for you?'

After introducing myself I said, 'Would you be good enough to assemble all the women so that I can talk to them?'

'Certainly I will, sir. If you'll wait here a few minutes I'll tell you when we're all present and correct.'

Five minutes later I was facing a room full of beautiful young women. In other circumstances I might have enjoyed the experience but now I had to do some serious talking. The brigadier called for silence and introduced me. As she was speaking I had a sudden idea about how some of these women could make themselves very useful. I decided that, first, I would tell them exactly what awaited them unless some action was taken. After that I'd seek volunteers from their number to solve a problem I'd been worrying about.

I began, 'Ladies, I am going to tell you why you are here. All but the very old men of this region have been conscripted into the Soviet Army. It is now the time of year for harvesting cotton and vegetables on the collective farms. The local women are busy collecting produce from the small plots on which they are allowed to grow crops for themselves. As winter approaches this harvesting is vitally important to them. If it is not done they and their children will starve.

The problem is that, while they are thus engaged, there is no-one to harvest the cotton crop. That is where you will come in. The women from the farms will come here – and it could be at any time now – and pick slaves from among your number, slaves to pick cotton in their stead. The working conditions will be atrocious. You will certainly be last in the queue for food.

My advice to you is to go from here as quickly as you can, and seek work for yourselves, either on the local farms or in the cotton factories. If you do this you will earn some money, not much but enough to live on. You will be relatively independent and when the Polish delegation arrives, as must happen sometime, they will find you and repatriate you. I will make sure the authorities hear about you and know your locations.'

I stopped speaking for a moment and watched the consternation spreading among the women. Then I went on, 'Personally I need ten or so women who can write neatly to come and work for me. I am looking for volunteers. Is anyone willing?'

I waited and two girls stepped forward. Then the brigadier did the same and she was immediately followed by about twenty more. I spoke to the rest.

'Thank you for listening to me so patiently. I hope you will do as I suggest without delay. I wish you all the best of luck.' The women drifted away chattering excitedly, and I turned to the volunteers. I chose the twelve who were most neatly dressed and, regretfully, sent the rest away. Those remaining included the brigadier.

'The NKVD is trying to lessen the congestion in Nukus,' I explained to the group. 'At the moment, those who want to join the Polish army are assembling around Farab, but the civilians are being evacuated to collective farms as far away as the Amu-Dar'ya delta and the Aral Sea. It is imperative that we try to list the names of those being deported and, if possible, the areas to which they are going. We must not lose track of our people. You are free to decide how best to go about the very difficult task of listing names and destinations. For safety you must work in twos. My suggestion is that you make as many barge trips as possible to and from Farab with the deportees. It may be possible for one of you to travel on the tugboat and be as charming as necessary to those in charge. Meanwhile, the other can move from one barge to the other during the journey, listing those on board. The lists must then be handed to the Polish Military Office which I am in the process of setting up in Nukus Port. Your work will be hard, possibly dangerous, and so will require courage as well as initiative. Are you all still willing to help?'

The brigadier looked round at the women and then back at me. 'We are,' she said.

'At the moment I can't help you financially but I will get food for you,' I explained. 'I can't even give you paper and pencils yet but I'll sort that out within the next couple of days.'

Later I travelled with the women over the river and found them somewhere to sleep.

The next day I was able to dispense with my 'sandal' and wear two shoes. I washed, shaved and made myself as smart as possible. It was time to approach the NKVD about food for my people. I was greeted by a young officer and, after introductions, I said, 'I need food for my transport. We've been surviving on our remaining dry rations since we arrived but those have now gone. I have been ill for a few days or I would have come to you earlier.'

'How many people travelled with you?' When I told him he said that the mess could provide soup and bread twice a day until the people were dispersed. He was pleasant and seemed well disposed towards me. I took a deep breath and launched the plan that I had made while I lay in the dark with my ulcerated leg. It was a plan that I hoped would prevent my being sent to a collective farm.

Casually I remarked, 'I often wonder if the NKVD officers have access to good meat. You're off the beaten track here. I suppose you have to make do with the same sort of food as we do.'

For a moment he looked suspicious and I wondered if I'd gone too far. Then he smiled ruefully, 'You're right. This posting is unpopular because of the quality of the food. We're right by the river but we never get decent fresh produce – just dry rubbish. Even our good cooks can't do much with it.'

'No salt pork or bacon?'

'Not likely. My mouth waters just thinking about it.'

'I happen to know that there are hundreds of wild pigs roaming the great marshes of the Amu Dar'ya delta, on the shores of the Aral Sea, in the Karakalpakia area.' I said. 'The locals are Muslims who don't eat pig meat. The only predators of the wild pigs are tigers. I also happen to know that I could easily raise a brigade of excellent marksmen, all experienced hunters. With your permission we could go and shoot the pigs, salt them and bring them back to grace the NKVD tables. What do you think?'
The officer was enthusiastic. 'You could really organise that?'

'*Certainly.*' *I felt things were going well.*

'*What would you need?*'

'*Twenty rifles with ammunition, food, barrels for storing the salted pork and a field kitchen. We'll find the salt for ourselves.*' *The officer looked serious for a moment.*

'*Obviously I can't take this decision on my own,*' *he said.* '*Leave it with me and I'll discuss it with my superiors. Come back and see me in – say three days' time. I'm sure I'll have good news for you then.*'

So far so good. I thought about what I'd do if my plan worked out – who I'd leave in charge of the people and the office I was about set up in a small shed near the quay.

I sought out a warrant officer from Vilno who had joined our transport in Farab. I knew he was a first-rate huntsman. When I told him what might be afoot he was delighted.

'*Count me in,*' *he said.*

'*I'm thinking of taking about twenty people in all,*' *I explained.* '*We need a cook, two people to wash and maintain our clothes which are falling apart, a quartermaster, a general orderly and fifteen marksmen. Don't tell anyone about this until we know for certain we can go. Just think about who might come with us – particularly anyone who's a good shot on the field.*'

I returned to the office, taking with me a lieutenant to whom I explained why I had set it up. '*New Polish arrivals will register here,*' *I said. I showed him how far the lists recording Polish people, already in Nukus, had progressed. They showed names, places of birth and latest addresses in Poland. I told him about the team of 'happy ladies' who would list people en route to collective farms. 'There's bound to be some duplication but we could rectify that as we go along and it will serve as some sort of check. I may have to go away for a while. If I do, I want you to take charge of the office.' I gave no hint of the anticipated hunting trip.*

Three days later I was back in the NKVD Office.

'Excellent news,' beamed the young officer. 'Your trip is on. Everyone thinks it's a wonderful idea.' I felt excitement surge inside me. I hadn't felt this good for a long time. The euphoria was modified somewhat when the officer went on, 'There is one problem, though. We have no spare rifles.'

'Do you expect us to catch wild pigs with our hands?' I asked incredulously.

He shrugged and repeated, 'We have no spare rifles.'

I thought quickly. I couldn't bear the thought of this beautiful idea being wasted. 'Have you any bierdanki?' (old fashioned, single shot carbines)

'Probably.'

'Those will do.'

'I'll find some. Don't hang around waiting for them. I'll have then delivered to you en route.' He handed me a piece of paper. 'Here is an order for you to present at the collective farms on your way. They will supply food, barrels for the pork and sleeping accommodation. The first will also give you a field kitchen. You will travel by tugboat, departing tomorrow. There will be food on the boat for times when you're not in reach of a collective farm. Be on the quay at 0800 hours to take a ferry across. Good luck.'

I could hardly believe everything was working out so well. I managed to obtain some paper and pencils for the 'happy ladies' and officially handed the office over to my Lieutenant.

The next day our twenty strong brigade crossed the river and waited for the tugboat to arrive. Small boats were coming and going all the time.

Suddenly a runner appeared from the direction of a newly arrived ferry. 'Message for Captain Dzierżiek.'

'I'm here,'

'Message from Polish Headquarters.' He passed me an official-looking envelope. I opened it to find that I had been appointed official Area Representative of the Polish Government and of the High Command of the Polish Army. My orders were to go to Farab and await further instructions. The news was bitter-sweet. I felt honoured and proud at my appointment, but sorely disappointed at being unable to participate in the hunting expedition. With regret, I waved the huntsmen off on the tugboat, having put the WO from Vilno in charge. I caught the next ferry back to Nukus Port.

The NKVD officer was surprised at my reappearance. He congratulated me when I showed him the letter and was pleased to hear the hunting brigade going ahead.

A few days later I was on my way back to Farab.

In January 1942, in Farab, I came across a Polish corporal who looked familiar. He recognised me immediately and saluted.

He had a fat stomach and I said, sympathetically, 'Are you swollen from malnutrition? Have you been very short of food?'

'Short of food? Certainly not Captain. Quite the reverse. I was in the hunting brigade you sent off to Karakalpakia. We're all this shape.'

'You were all good shots then?'

'We never found that out, Captain. The carbines didn't arrive. The collective farms refused us food and accommodation and wouldn't give us barrels or a field kitchen. However, when we arrived on the plain the W.O. fixed everything. He made friends with the locals who showed us how to build a ziemianka (sunken mud hut). From the outside it looked like a hump but inside it was roomy, comfortable and well insulated. Then we dug deep trenches, covered them with reeds, and trapped wild pigs which we killed and salted. We made nets and caught ducks and wild geese for a change in our diet. We exchanged some of the meat for cereals and other necessities at the nearest collective farm. We made sausages and exchanged these at the local Russian town for vegetables and sugar. We lived like kings and got on well with all our neighbours. I'm here in Farab to ask you what our group should do now. Shall we stay where we are or shall we come back here and await orders?'

I couldn't help smiling at the thought of the little group of pioneer hunters. I gave the Corporal three days' R and R then supplied him with food and sent him back to close the hunting enterprise down and report back to Farab with the rest of his brigade. Shooting had always been my favourite sport. How I would have loved to have been part of that hunting party!

Shooting Ducks

It is my turn to choose a photograph at the start of the lesson. Dziadek smiles as he looks through his magnifying glass at a picture of my seven-month-old granddaughter, Joy, in the little swing suspended in the doorway of the living room. He is in the photo too, with his stick at the ready to push the swing.

Dziadek and Joy Jr

He seems to like it when my family come to see him. He and my mother, who is a mere eighty five, will sometimes sit side by side on the settee, quietly watching the children. They have become fond of each other. Mum is enchanted by Dziadek's gallantry – with the way he always struggles to his feet to greet her and kiss her hand.

In the photos he shows me of himself with his own daughter he never appears to be comfortable, but he seems to relax with my three grandchildren. He'll happily nurse Joy and try to engage Isobel, who is nearly four, in conversation. She won't be drawn, however.

She will lurk by the door, rush in, shout 'Hello Dziadek' and then scuttle away. She confesses that she's 'a bit frightened of his whiskers and funny voice.'

Now as he smiles over the photograph of Joy, in the stick-propelled swing, he caresses the top of his walking stick absent-mindedly. I know how important that stick is to him. I remember the occasion the previous year when he, Danka, Isobel and I took the dog to Wandsworth Common. Dziadek wasn't in a wheelchair then and enjoyed a slow wander round the pond. He stopped now and then to peer down into the restless water where carp were spawning, fingering his stick as if it were a fishing rod. Then suddenly he looked skyward, raised the stick, took aim and 'shot' one of the ducks which flew overhead. He had slipped into another time – he was back on his family's country estate. Meanwhile, Isobel and I were inhabiting a totally different reality. Isobel (Christopher Robin) and I (Winnie the Pooh) were in the 'Hundred Acre Wood' having exciting adventures which included high branches and honey pots. Our world and Dziadek's ran parallel and neither impinged upon the other.

A year on in Cheshire, Dziadek is still shooting ducks. After the lesson Danka and I take him and Isobel to the park. He is in his wheelchair and Isobel is trotting alongside. As we walk towards the children's playground some ducks fly overhead. In a trice Dziadek cocks his stick, takes aim and fires, shouting 'Bang!' so loudly that we all jump. This amuses him so much that he 'shoots' a couple of unsuspecting pigeons too. This is the nearest he can get to his favourite country sport.

On our way home from the park as we cross the main road to the supermarket he holds his stick aloft as if to halt the traffic. 'Cars see stick, they stop!' he cries. Fortunately, as we are using a pelican crossing we don't have to put his theory to the test. The supermarket is crowded so I stand outside with Isobel, but he insists that Danka takes him in. I watch him through the window with his stick held straight out in front as if he is a warrior charging into battle. Other customers leap aside and the aisle ahead of him clears as he disappears from my view.

Later I learn that his walking stick served him very well on one occasion. He was in his late eighties at the time, and on his way to the Polish Church in Tooting. Three youths leapt from behind a hedge and demanded his wallet. He tried to ignore them and walk on but one grabbed him. He lashed out with his walking stick and the boy yelped and let go. Then, using his stick like a sword he beat off the other muggers. They scattered and Dziadek managed to get to the church on time.

November – December 1941

We travelled from Nukus to Farab by barge. I took Jagielski and an Aide with me. We arrived in the evening. There was no-one to meet us although I knew the NKVD had been apprised of our arrival. We looked for somewhere to sleep and ended up in the port buildings. We slept on tables.

Early the next morning I managed to wash and shave in the toilet area. After a small breakfast of dry rations I went to find the NKVD Commander. As I lifted my hand to knock the door a lieutenant emerged. 'What do you want?' he demanded.

'My business is with the major,' I said. 'I am a captain in the Polish Army. Tell the major I wish to speak to him.' He didn't reply but went back into the office, slamming the door.

After a few minutes he came out and jerked his head in the direction of the office.

'Go in.'

I entered and found the major sitting behind his desk. He had his hat on, jacket undone, and had kicked off his shoes. 'What do you want?' he asked in an aggressive tone.

'I have come to thank you for your hospitality.' I replied. 'Last night I slept on a table in the port waiting room.' He tried to interrupt but I went on. 'In 1939, when I was in the Frontier Guard even the humblest peasant was offered a bed if he asked for help and it was too late for him to find accommodation. Officers were shown to the nearest hotel and no expense was spared. That is Polish hospitality. I think you will agree that it is of a higher standard than that offered by the Soviet people.'

The major leapt up. 'You insolent...' He didn't get any further because I put my documents into his hand. He glanced down, saw my rank and then took a closer look. I was described as

"Commander", and although he was a major and I was only a captain, my actual position, my post, was higher than his. As had happened so many times before, in similar situations, I saw an instant change in the man's attitude.

He took off his hat and buttoned his jacket as he spoke. 'Comrade Captain, there has been a great misunderstanding, I apologise for this. I haven't yet received any information about your arrival. I'll do all in my power to rectify the situation. Please be seated.' He opened the door and ordered his Lieutenant to find quarters for me.

'I have another officer and an Aide with me,' I said.

'There will be accommodation for them too, of course.' The major couldn't do enough for me.

'This is incredible,' I thought, as I remembered the prisons and labour camps where torture was the norm, where I had felt stripped of all dignity and self-worth. Now my identity and selfhood were being slowly restored as I interacted with the very same people who had taken it away.

'Please follow me sir. I know of some suitable quarters.' I was jolted from my reverie by the lieutenant, now smiling.

'I'll come too,' said the major. 'Just to make sure they are good enough.'

It was a large room furnished with a strange collection of items. There was a metal-framed bed with a straw mattress, sheets, blankets and pillows. There was a big wooden table, three odd chairs, two mismatched stools and a small cupboard. The major gave a little laugh of embarrassment, 'We military men don't look for comfort do we?' he said.

'Somewhere to wash would be nice,' I remarked hopefully.

'Of course,' and to the lieutenant, 'Arrange that with the landlady at once.' He turned to me again. Tell me where your luggage is and I'll send someone to fetch it.'

'My luggage is what I'm wearing. My spare clothes, shoes, cigarette box, signet ring and a sum of money were left in Lithuanian Minsk Prison when I was moved. It's all still in storage there.'

The major was put out by the implied criticism. 'You'll get it back, you'll get it back,' he blustered. 'It's the fault of the war. Nobody can be held responsible.'

I spent the next couple of days establishing a Polish Military 'Office'. It was, in fact, a disused cold drinks kiosk with a small adjoining shed. But at least it was shelter from the worst of the weather. This office would serve the same purpose as the one I'd opened in Nukus – that of listing and trying to keep track of the thousands of Poles who were constantly passing through the transit camp. Also we would issue meal coupons to new arrivals.

I was on my way to the office on the second day, when I encountered Stanislav Świetlik. He was standing in front of a battalion of what I took, at first, to be soldiers. They were fully uniformed in belted coats and high, shining boots, but were wearing hats of the Polish Police Reserve. As I watched, the leader of the battalion moved forward to deliver a report to the civilian stationed at the front, who didn't seem to know how to stand while receiving it. The leader then dismissed the policemen and I approached the civilian and introduced myself. I was curious about what I'd just witnessed so I asked to see his papers.

'I've only got my release papers from the labour camp,' he said and handed them to me. 'Actually I am a captain in the regular Polish police force. I was recently in Dzhizak where I was involved in assembling men who had been working on collective farms and wanted to join the army. The leader of this Battalion asked me if I could arrange transport so that the men could join up with the Polish army. I was told Farab was the place to come so I negotiated with the NKVD, for them to supply transport to get us here. Now we're here, there's no sign of the army and the local NKVD is refusing to supply food for us, saying no-one gave advance notice of our arrival.'

'Give me a couple of hours to sort something out,' I said. 'Keep your efficient army out of sight, meanwhile. I think the NKVD finds it intimidating. My office is over there. I'll see you at about midday.'

As I turned to retrace my steps to the NKVD office I hit on a plan. I apologised to the major for bothering him again so soon, and then asked him, 'Have you seen the Police Army we have in our midst?'

'I have. I can't think why they've been sent here. I know there's no room in Buzuluk or in Nukus. The same is probably true of Jangi-Jul, where your army's headquarters are now, even though I gather they're erecting temporary buildings as fast as they can. Having said that, there's certainly no room here either. It's a real dilemma.'

I knew I must try to make the major think that he, himself, had thought of my plan.

'I wonder if they should go back to Dzhizak,' I said.

'Exactly what I was thinking.'

'Do you think it would be possible for them to be placed together, on a large collective farm near Dzhizak? Then they could continue training and when the time is right...'

'They could join up with the Polish Army.' He finished my sentence for me and the job was done. He gave me a written order to give to Świetlik. He promised transport at 0800 hours the next morning and food for the journey. There was a spring in my step as I went to my office. I had good news for Świetlik.

My next task was to check the mess kitchen and the one at the railway station. Neither was functioning properly. I asked Jagielski to gather suitable people from our transport to appoint leaders and instigate a thorough clean.

Then I set out to see Chairman Comrade Szmidt, the civilian in charge of the area in which I was based. He agreed to supply food and shelter for my people. He also insisted on providing curtains and crockery for my room.

One evening, after a particularly difficult day, I was locking the door of the office when a strange small figure limped into view. I was turning away when I heard my name.

'Please Captain, may I speak to you.' She looked like an urchin. Her clothes were ragged and stained but her voice was that of a well-educated Polish lady. There was nothing unusual in that. There were many such in Farab. War is no respecter of rank.

I sighed. I would help her if I could – but not tonight. *'I'm sorry, my office is closed. Please come back tomorrow.'*

She didn't move but opened her large, dark eyes wide. *'Sir, my name is Anna Grzymała Siedlecka. I have just arrived in Farab. I'm alone and have no money and no friends. I'm cold and I'm nervous about being out in the open all night. I apologise for bothering you but I'm in desperate need of help.'*

For a moment I was overwhelmed by a feeling of despair. There were hundreds of people in a similar position to this young woman. I simply could not help them all, however hard I worked. But I could find something for her to eat now and some shelter for the night.

I opened my mouth to speak but she seemed to interpret my pause as indifference, for she spun round and walked rapidly down the street, her head in the air.

Astonished, I shouted, *'Where do you think you're going?'* She stopped and turned back, then she walked slowly towards me, saying nothing. *'How do you come to be here and how do you know who I am?'* I asked.

'I was with your group in Tashkent. I went with the others to Nukus, but I really want to join the Polish Army and there seemed no chance of doing it there so I came back to Farab on my own.'

'An independent and hot-headed young woman,' I thought as I unlocked the office door. *'I haven't much to give you tonight, I'm afraid,'* I said. She accepted the dry bread and warm water gratefully enough, although there was something in her attitude which made me feel that she was doing me the favour rather than the other way round. When she had finished I directed her to a waiting-hall at the port building where I knew many women would be sleeping. She'd be relatively safe there.

Early the next morning she was, again, at my office door. She looked cleaner; had fresh foot wrappings and a scarf on.

'Thank you very much for the food and help you gave me last night,' she began. 'While I'm waiting for orders to join the army do you think there is any chance of my finding temporary work in Farab? I'll do anything at all. I just need to earn some money so that I can support myself.'

I almost laughed aloud. Temporary work? Where did she think she was – in Warsaw in peace time? Then a thought struck me. She might just prove useful in the office.

'Do you speak Russian?' She flushed and answered me as if I should have known better than to ask such a question.

'Yes sir, I do. And I speak English, French and Ukrainian.' Then, with thinly veiled sarcasm, 'And I can write, count and even type.'

I smiled. 'Yes, she might well be useful,' I thought, but I also felt I should explain the situation to her. 'You do realise this is a transit point, don't you? People come here to be transported to whichever destinations seem appropriate. Currently the Polish Army has stopped all recruitment, and most Poles are being sent to collective farms or factories. Because I represent the Polish Government, I'm allowed to retain a small staff here. It has to be small – the NKVD is always counting.'

I could see how disappointed she was. She struggled to keep her voice steady. 'Thank you for explaining things to me, Captain.' Then, very coldly, 'I won't bother you further. Please just tell me which transport I should join and I'll leave immediately.' To my surprise, and without waiting for an answer, she once more turned her back on me and hurried away.

I called my young lieutenant and pointed to Anna's fast disappearing figure and told him her name. 'Run after her,' I instructed. 'Bring her back to the office.'

She came through the door reluctantly. 'What a hothead you are,' I exclaimed. 'Do you always leave in the middle of a conversation? I'm afraid I can't offer you a permanent position here, but if you'd like to stay and work here for the time being, I'll persuade the NKVD that we really need your skills. There will be *a small remuneration and I'm sure we'll be able to sort some lodgings out for you too.'*

Anna proved efficient and competent. She was even prepared to help with the identification and burial of the corpses of the men, women and children who had died en route to Farab. She was small in stature but determined and resilient.

My office became increasingly busy. One arrival was a Polish priest. He had with him a portable altar. We converted my room into a church at specified times each day. The priest gave attendees blue plastic crucifixes which were highly prized. We even had a christening of a young boy, brought in by his grandmother. She asked me to be godfather.

At last an orderly came, from Jangi-Jul, with a full British uniform for me.
'There's certainly growing room,' I laughed as I tried it on.
'Don't worry,' Jagielski said, 'I know of a tailor in our midst. I'll ask him to alter it for you.' The tailor did me proud. When I looked at my reflection in a window the next day I thanked him warmly.
I couldn't remember when I had last looked so smart.

Eventually my pay arrived from Headquarters. Now my appearance was no longer shabby and I had money in my pocket. I treated myself to a new watch. Then I decided that it was time to report to the Head Office of the NKVD in Czardzou. In fact, I should have done so sooner, considering my position as Representative of both the Polish Army and Polish Government.

I had no problem gaining an interview with the NKVD general. 'At last,' he said, after introductions. 'I've been wondering why no-one from the Farab's Polish contingent has been to see me.'
'I hadn't anything to wear, your honour. As soon as I received my uniform I came.'

'How are you managing in Farab?' he asked. 'My major there is a difficult man.' I assured him that I was being looked after very well. We discussed the overcrowded conditions in Farab, the dispersals to collective farms and the necessity for more food for the people in transit.

'I'll do what I can to help,' he assured me. Our meeting lasted almost two hours and I left Czardzou feeling satisfied that I had done everything possible for my people.

Back in Farab, the first person I met was the 'difficult' major. He was very anxious to know what had happened during my meeting with his superior. 'What did the general want to know? Did he ask about your quarters? Is he likely to visit us in the near future?' I assured him that the general had seemed pleased with what I told him. Seizing the advantage, I suggested something I had had in mind for some time – something to ease congestion in Farab and bring about some sort of order out of the chaos.

'I have discussed the problem of overcrowding with the general,' I said. 'We both feel that priority for food and shelter should be given to those people who have been recently released from prison or labour camps. Next in line should be those who have travelled here from far distant collective farms. The people who are from local farms, however, should be sent back for the moment. On the farms they'll get food and shelter. We will record where everyone goes so that they can be contacted when the time comes. What do you think of this idea?' In view of the general's apparent endorsement of my plan, he could only agree.

When I went to the office I was surprised to find that Anna was no longer working there. Another woman had taken her place. I questioned Lieutenant B., whom I had left in charge. 'That woman is a troublemaker,' he replied. 'As soon as you left for Czardzou she was up to all sorts of tricks. She came in late and told lies about the others in the office. I thought it best to get rid of her.' I felt a stab of disappointment. Anna had let me down. But there wasn't time to think further about it. There was too much to do.

The next day I was accosted by Anna as I turned into the street leading to my office.

'Excuse me sir,' she said, 'You'll know that I was dismissed by Lieutenant B., while you were away. He gave me no explanation. I'm not asking for my job back, but I've no money so I must work. I'll go to a kolkhoz (collective farm) if necessary. But first, will you please tell me the reason for my dismissal?'

Suddenly I lost patience with this impudent slip of a girl. Who did she think she was – storming off, questioning, criticising? I had too many responsibilities to allow myself to be side-tracked by her. 'My dear girl,' I said icily, 'We'll probably all be sent to kolkhozes soon. Who knows what the future holds? My officer was entitled to dismiss you if he deemed it necessary. I don't have to explain his decision to you.' She stood in front of me, red with anger and, although I didn't repent of what I'd said, I couldn't simply let her leave with no money at all. I had only a twenty-five rouble note with me. I held it out to her. 'Report to the railway station at 6 a.m. tomorrow. A transport is leaving then.'

Anna ignored the bank note. 'I am not a beggar, Captain. I don't want your money. I will leave Farab – but in my own time, when I'm ready.' Her voice was cold. Then she said something which was to come back to haunt me. 'I hope that one day we'll meet in different circumstances, and that by then, you'll have realised how unfairly you've treated me. I hope that you will apologise to me then.' With that she stalked past me and away.

Things in Farab improved for a while, as a result of my discussion with the NKVD general. Then there was a sudden influx of transports. Food became very scarce once more. Worried, I knew I must do something else. I obtained a pass to visit a Polish Minister in Tashkent.

He received me courteously, 'Thank you for all you are doing under difficult circumstances.' he said. 'Is there anything I can do to help?'

'I've come to ask if you would use your influence to stop the Authorities from directing transports of Polish refugees to Farab,

please sir. Overcrowding is so bad that, not only is it impossible to feed everyone properly, but I am seriously worried about the danger of an outbreak of typhus.' The minister promised to do all he could.

I was very surprised when he suddenly said, 'And now may I ask you to do me a favour? There is to be a big ball tomorrow night at the best hotel in Tashkent. It's a sort of "Hail and Farewell" celebration. Some Polish officers have just arrived and the Russian officers who have been stationed here are moving on.' I listened politely, unable to see what this had to do with me. The minister went on, 'My dark suit is so threadbare that I fear it won't hold together if I wear it to the ball. I have nothing else suitable to wear. You, on the other hand, are extremely smart in your uniform. Would you be prepared to go instead of me?'

Thus, the following evening I found myself with a lovely lady on my arm, in the vestibule of a fine hotel. I've never forgotten the sight that met my eyes when the double doors of the splendid dining room were thrown open. In the centre was an enormous dining table, spread with a gleaming cloth, on which shimmered silver cutlery and crystal goblets. Waiters, clad in black and wearing white gloves, showed us to our places and stood behind the chairs ready to serve us the first course; soup, the like of which I had not tasted since before the war. An orchestra, seated on a podium at one end of the room, played softly as I marvelled at this turn of events. Not so long ago I was hungry and ragged, and here I was enjoying the best of everything. It felt unreal – which it was, of course. Reality lay among the hosts of my people back in Farab.

Suddenly I noticed a long table set in an alcove at the far end of the room. Sitting at the table, which was covered with worn and torn oilcloth, sat a group of senior Soviet officers, all shabbily dressed; a sorry sight. I realised that they were probably guests in residence at the hotel – guests who had not been invited to this prestigious ball. Their only cutlery was a well-used knife which was fastened by a chain to the centre of the table. Soup was being ladled into metal canteens in front of them. They were forced to lift these and drink the soup without the services of a spoon. Suddenly a NKVD officer appeared and went over to them. 'Hurry up! Finish quickly and leave the room. Come on!' The colonels, majors and even a general rose from the table, whether or not they had finished their soup, and trooped out silently with never a backward glance. It was an incredible sight. The NKVD Officer turned to the Master of Ceremonies with a small bow. 'From this moment only invited guests will be allowed into the room.' Then he addressed all of us. 'You, ladies and gentlemen, will be served with the best of everything. After you have eaten the tables will be pushed aside so that you may dance. The orchestra will play for as long as you wish. I hope you all have a wonderful evening.' With that he left the room and the atmosphere lightened.

My partner and I enjoyed each other's company very much. We had a good deal in common and laughed and talked until the delicious meal was over. Then we danced, allowing all our anxieties to flow away as the orchestra played. We walked back to the minister's house together, in the crisp cold moonlight. It had certainly been an evening to remember.

The next day, before I returned to Farab, the minister received a parcel of food as a consolation for his absence from the banquet. He insisted on sharing it with me, so I carried away two boxes of sardines, some cheese, a Russian sausage, a packet of tea and a few sweetmeats. I felt I'd done very well out of my trip to Tashkent.

When I arrived back in the office I found everything in disarray. The young officer met me with the news that he had discovered that the woman who had replaced Anna had been selling the meal tickets for her own gain.

'And Lieutenant B., was he in on it?' I demanded. The young man looked down.

'I'm afraid so sir. They were having an affair.' The face of Anna Grzymała Siedlecka swam before me, and her words, "...you'll have realised how unfairly you've treated me..."

echoed in my ears. What had I done? I'd never forgive myself if anything happened to her as a result of my intransigence. I knew I'd have to deal with Lieutenant B., but that could wait for the moment. I must try to right the wrong I had done. I told the officer the address of Anna's lodgings.

'Go there straight away,' I said. 'Ask her to come to the office immediately'. Within ten minutes he was back.

'She's gone, sir. The landlady said she took her belongings and went to the railway station a few days ago.'

I asked him for the list of people who had left Farab while I was away. And there was her name. She had left for Bukhara three days ago. By now she had probably been allocated to a kolkhoz in the Bukhara area. I might never see her again.

There was no time to brood. The ball in Tashkent had given me an idea. Obviously I couldn't organise anything on such a scale, but I could give a small party in my room. It would be especially for Chairman Szmidt and would be a means of my obtaining a better deal for the Polish people A fellow lodger promised to play the harmonium and my landlady said she'd lend me crockery, a tablecloth and wine glasses. I had the food from the minister's parcel and I managed to obtain some more cheese and bread as well as several bottles of vodka.

The Chairman was delighted with his invitation and arrived early. His face lit up at the spread on the table and, with a flourish, he pulled another bottle of vodka from his pocket. I had taken the precaution of swallowing a couple of spoons full of oil from the sardines before he arrived so I knew I would stay reasonably sober if I were careful. My guest was not careful. Before long he was dancing round the table and singing loudly to the accompaniment of the harmonium. Finally he leapt so high that he lost his footing and fell on to the wooden floor, hitting his head hard. He lay still. 'Oh God, I've killed the Chairman,' I thought, but he gave a moan and I knew he was alive. Jagielski ran for help from the First Aid Office. I called my landlady who brought water and towels. Within minutes the Chairman was *carried out on a stretcher and taken to hospital. I had some vodka to calm my nerves.*

The next day I visited Szmidt in the hospital. He had a very sore head but didn't hold it against me. 'I had a wonderful time,' he said. 'It was so kind of you to throw a party especially for me. No-one has ever done that before.'

I felt happy at the way things were turning out. I was satisfied that my people were as safe and well fed as was possible in those tumultuous times. Christmas 1941 was the best for me since the start of the war. Szmidt gave sweets and iced ginger biscuits to all Polish children, and released a little more food so that on Christmas Eve, we managed a modest traditional celebration. I had bought some fabric decorations from a local woman and we even had a small decorated tree.

Then in the New Year I was presented with an even greater challenge.

Two Festivals and a Walk

Dziadek with his wife and daughter.

I feel sure the photograph doesn't do justice to a glorious Christmas tree; for Dziadek glows with pride as he shows it to me. 'I do all,' he explains. 'I find, I put here' – pointing to its base – 'I put on.' Here he points to the decorations suspended from the tree. Clearly the tradition of having a tree at Christmas is extremely important to him. Indeed, I discover that it holds a special place in the hearts of all Polish people.

Each year, 'in the old days' just before Christmas, Dziadek would go into the forest and cut down a pine tree. In Manchester and later in London, he went to the local markets and chose the tallest, straightest, best shaped tree he could afford. He would conceal it outside until Christmas Eve when he banished everyone else from the living room, brought it inside and fixed it into the wooden stand he had made for the purpose. He had already retrieved the precious boxes of tree decorations and lights from the loft. Some of the decorations had come from Farab. Dziadek had met a woman selling the shiny fabric baubles for a few zlotys and had bought them in an act of defiance, determined that he would live to celebrate a traditional Christmas at home once more. They had remained hidden in his kit until he arrived in England, where they graced his tree each year. The large coloured tree lights dated from 1948.

Now, on Christmas Eve he shuts the door so that he can be alone to perform the decorating ceremony. Nobody will be allowed to see the tree until just before the special meal.

The year I was invited to participate in the Christmas Eve feast I was shown into the living room where I admired the tree. Then we went into a small dining room. The table, which almost filled it, was spread with a white lace tablecloth covered with a delicious array of food. There were dishes of pasties, pickled and salted fish and salads. Five places were laid although only four of us were present. 'It's traditional to lay an extra place,' Anna explained, 'in case an unexpected visitor arrives or a stranger knocks on our door. No-one is turned away on Christmas Eve.'

Before we sat down Dziadek picked up two pieces of a wafer from the table. In keeping with another Polish tradition, he had sent half of one wafer to his family in Poland and they had sent half of theirs to him. We now shared these halves at approximately the same time as the relatives in Poland would be sharing the halves they had – a symbol of unity in spite of the miles that lay between. First Dziadek broke off two small pieces, handed one to Anna and ate one himself. He then kissed her on both cheeks and said 'Wesolych Swiat' ('Happy Christmas') and she reciprocated. He moved round the table, repeating the ritual with Danka and me. Anna did the same and so on until each of us had shared a morsel of wafer with everyone else. Next we exchanged Christmas presents. Only then did we sit down. Anna brought in a tureen of clear, claret-coloured beetroot soup and the feast began.

In my ignorance I assumed that what was on the table was the sum total of the meal. Dish after dish was handed to me and when I felt I could eat no more Dziadek said, 'Now hot fish.' Dismayed, I managed to struggle through a small helping of baked fish and vegetables but failed at the desert course of kutia/kootya, kompot and kisiel.

In fact the meal comprised twelve dishes, symbolising the twelve apostles. Silently I vowed that if I were invited to another such Feast, I would pace myself.

Every year, after Christmas, there was dissension between Anna and Dziadek about how long the Christmas tree should be allowed to remain indoors. The latter had been raised in the Russian Orthodox tradition. Ideally he would have liked to celebrate Christmas on the 6th January. Failing that, he insisted on keeping the decorated tree until 18th January, Orthodox Twelfth Night. Only once did he manage to hang on to it until 'The Feast of the Virgin' in February, and that was when Anna had gone away for a few weeks. No-one was ever allowed to help with the dismantling of the brown and balding tree. Each beloved decoration was carefully wrapped in tissue paper, boxed and stowed, with regret, in the attic ready for next Christmas.

Easter brought another ceremony which Dziadek took equally seriously. Some time during the week before Easter he went to the local Polish shop and selected three dozen large white eggs. At home he carefully scrubbed them, placed them in pans of water and vinegar and hard boiled them. The vinegar, he alleged, removed any residue of grease and minimised leakage should one of the eggs crack. While the eggs were boiling Dziadek covered the dining table with newspaper on which he placed some tea towels, a dozen or so strips of cotton cloth, five jam jars in each of which stood a spoon, five small packets of dye, and the vinegar. He mixed a dye in each jar by pouring boiling water over the spoon and mixing briskly. A tablespoonful of vinegar was then added to help 'set' the dye. By now the eggs would be ready. He dried them, lined them up and then dipped each, in turn, into a dye, turning it for even colouring. Some he left in for some time – for deep colouration. Others were lifted out quickly.Thus a variety of shades was achieved. The dyed eggs were placed on the cotton strips and while they dried Dziadek cut pieces of greenery from the garden and arranged them in several dishes and small baskets. The final task was to rub olive oil on to the eggs which were then placed, lovingly, into the dishes and baskets where, jewel-like, they gleamed.

On Easter Saturday Dziadek chose the best basket of eggs, added to it some yeast cake, a traditional Polish confection for Easter, and covered everything with a spotless, freshly ironed, white table napkin. Proudly he bore his creation to church where he placed it on the altar steps alongside similar baskets brought by other members of the congregation. Then, at a special service, the priest gave his blessing to the food.

When Dziadek arrived home from church and the family sat down to eat, they started by sharing one of the 'blessed eggs' as an act of communion and unity.

The Easter after he moved to Cheshire, Dziadek was not too well and couldn't make the journey to the Polish Church for the blessing of the eggs that he and Danka had so painstakingly dyed. He was very quiet and Danka guessed he was fretting. On an impulse she phoned the local priest, a young Irishman. Mystified by her request he nevertheless came straight away. When he understood the significance of the ritual he was delighted to bless the basket of Polish food and even more delighted to be invited to stay and share the family meal which followed.

The Polish Group, Manchester Whit walk 1951.

When Dziadek lived in Manchester there was a third important event on his calendar – the Whit Walk. With pleasure he showed me photographs of the Polish contingent at the Walk and then, almost shyly, one of himself dressed for the parade, in the costume of an eighteenth century Polish nobleman.

Dziadek as an eighteenth century Polish nobleman

'First years I hire from dancers,' he explains. 'Then I ask lady make it.'

Manchester was drab, its buildings grimy in the post war years – what an exotic splash the parades from the various churches and international groups must have made. The Poles walked between the Irish and the Italians. The Irish, in their brown and green, were accompanied by 'The Brian Borhu Pipe Band'. Their children, heads held high, hands behind them, walked in time to the music - like dancers. The Italians, in national costume bore aloft a beautiful Madonna, framed in lilies. But, 'Polish best,' Dziadek told me with a smile. Their costumes with shiny beads, buttons, flowers and ribbons were augmented by a huge and striking Black Madonna, held high by four men.

As Dziadek gazed at the old photographs, I glimpsed for a moment his intense national pride and was moved by the thought that the Whit Walks had afforded him a rare opportunity in his post-war life, to express this pride and to be acknowledged for what he was and what he had done. He and all his Polish ex-service colleagues had been prevented from joining the victory parade along the Mall in 1946, for fear of offending Stalin. And it was not until the 1990s that Polish ex-service men and women were finally allowed to march with those of the Allies in the Remembrance Day Parade at Whitehall. By then, Dziadek was too old and infirm to take his place alongside his compatriots.

January 1942

What's the good of us being released from the camps only to die of starvation here?' an angry man shouted at me.

'We came here to join the army but no-one takes any notice of us,' shrieked another.

'Wish I'd stayed on the farm. At least there was food there,' roared a third.

The theme was taken up by others around.

I tried to shout above the noise. 'I've only just arrived in Bukhara. I'll go in to see...' My voice was drowned by shouts of derision. I was jostled and I struggled to stay upright.

Help came from an unexpected quarter. 'Listen to the Captain. Give him a chance!' a man bellowed. He hoisted himself up on to a wall and, for a moment, he had everyone's attention. 'These fellows here and I know this officer. He performed miracles in Farab. He fed us and found shelter for us. You can trust him to do his very best for us here as well.'

I was so moved that I could hardly respond. I nodded my thanks to him and managed to speak firmly and loudly. 'I am in the same position as you. I haven't eaten today. I have nowhere to sleep tonight. I shall now go to see the Polish Representative. I will report back to you all as soon as I can.'

It was 9th January 1942 and I had just arrived at Bukhara, by order of Polish High Command. Jagielski was with me. The Chairman at Farab had not been at all pleased when I told him I was leaving. 'I can't believe they're transferring you just when we're getting on so well and you've got everything organised.' He was almost petulant.

'I'm really very sorry to go,' I replied. 'But I'm happy in the knowledge that you will continue to care for my people for the sake of our friendship.'

'I certainly will,' he assured me, and I believed him. He knew I would receive regular reports of how things were in Farab and, for some reason, he was always keen that I should think well of him. Shaking his hand, I hurried out to brief the Polish officers to whom I would hand over my duties.

On arriving at Bukhara we had made our way to the office of Mr Młodzianowski, the civilian representative of the Polish Government in the city. We'd stopped in astonishment when we reached the courtyard in front of the office building. It was crowded to the extent that not a centimetre of paving was visible. The large garden, which was on three sides of the building, was the same. The street outside was thronging with Polish people begging for food. That was when, seeing my uniform, a large group of frustrated and disillusioned men had turned on me.

In the silence that followed my promise to see the Polish representative I pushed my way to the door.

I was admitted immediately because of my British uniform and soon found myself in Mr Młodzianowski's office.

After introductions I explained my errand. 'People are dying of hunger outside, as I'm sure you know,' I said. 'It's been snowing and there's no shelter. Can you do anything about the situation?'

He sat down heavily. 'What can I do?' he asked helplessly. 'I've very little money or accommodation at my disposal. Any food I can get hold of I send outside for the children. I daren't show my own face for fear of being lynched. Quite honestly, I'm at my wits end.' I realised I wouldn't get much out of him.

'If I can sort something out for those who want to join the army – and that seems to be the majority of the people outside – can I leave you to look after the civilians?' I asked him.

'I'll do my very best. Do you really think you can manage the military aspect?'

'I'll do my very best,' I echoed, shaking his hand. Later I heard that his wife has died on that very day, and I felt guilty about my impatience.

Outside the crowd was restless. I was concerned that I had nothing positive to tell them. 'The Polish representative and I are going to help you. It may take a couple of days but I promise things will get better,' I started.

'A couple of days?' There was general uproar. 'We'll have starved by then.'

'Let him get started on a solution, then,' shouted the man who had came to my rescue earlier. I left Jagielski to keep an eye on things while I went to explore the city and to search for accommodation for our potential recruits.

After walking for over two hours and seeing nothing at all suitable, I suddenly came across what seemed to be an enormous deserted barracks on the outskirts of the town. A guard appeared at the gate straight away. He was about to challenge me when he noticed my uniform, snapped to attention, saluted and then asked, 'What can I do to help you, sir?'

'Who is in charge of these barracks?' I asked.

'A Garrison Commander, sir.'

'Where is he now?'

'At barracks to the east of the city.' He gave me directions; I thanked him, turned and walked quickly the way he had indicated.

I discovered that the Garrison Commander was one of the old school. An elderly colonel, who had once served in the Tsar's Army. He listened to me sympathetically.

'Most of the men in the crowd are eager to fight alongside the Allies,' I concluded. 'If they are not found food and shelter soon, many will die and the condition of the rest will deteriorate so that they will be useless – or there will be a riot. The best way forward is to recruit them into the Polish Army. We could put them in the disused barracks where they can begin training straight away.'

He thought for a moment. In suspense, I held my breath. 'I'm inclined to agree,' he replied. I exhaled slowly as he went on, 'If they are in training the NKVD will provide food for them. I can organise that. Would you be prepared to be the chairman of the Recruitment Committee?'

'Thank you for doing me the honour of asking, but you as Garrison Commander should be in charge, sir.' He looked pleased and said,

'You shall be deputy chairman. I'll find a doctor to undertake the medicals. When do you want to start recruiting and where shall we hold the sessions?'

'I suggest we ask Mr Młodzianowski for the use of a room in his building. I'll go back and tell the people about our plans. I'll put a notice on the door too. We'll start tomorrow morning at 0900 hours, if that suits you. Can you enlist two or three more to the committee by then, do you think?'

'I can. I'll see you then. You'd better go. You've a lot to do.'

Within a few days every Polish man who wanted to join the army was settled in the barracks. Within a week all suitable and willing Poles in the surrounding area had joined them. The training began, but best of all, or so I thought, the NKVD was providing all the food we required.

February – Spring 1942

By February 1942, the soldiers occupying the barracks were training daily. Most of the civilians who were fit enough had gone to work on collective farms where they would be fed and housed for the time being – until the wretched war was over and we could all return to our homeland. Walking from my office one day, I met the Soviet colonel whose troops had once occupied the barracks. He seemed to know who I was and introduced himself. 'I am very pleased to meet you at last,' he said. 'I've been away but now I have resumed my duties, one of which is to inspect all parts of the compound regularly.'

'Do you want to inspect the barracks?' I enquired.

'I have already done so, thank you, and very pleased I am too. The dormitories are spick and span. Everything's in order. I even tasted the food which is excellent. Congratulations to you and to the officer directly in charge of the men.'

I thanked him and was about to move off when he gave a little cough. 'Ahem, I'm sorry to have to raise this matter but it is almost time for me to send in my quarterly report. I have to account for all the money spent. A good deal of money has been spent on feeding your Polish soldiers and on keeping their barracks warm, I'm afraid.' He looked embarrassed as he pulled a piece of paper from his pocket and looked at it. 'Five thousand roubles to be precise.'

'The Polish Army owes you five thousand roubles?'

'I'm afraid so.'

'But I understood that the NKVD would supply free food for our soldiers because they will be joining the Allied Forces.'

'Sorry, no. Rules have changed.'

I didn't know what to say. I had no budget and I wasn't sure how my superiors would react to such a demand.

'The best thing I can do is to go to the Polish Military Headquarters in Jangi-Jul. I'll go tomorrow and explain the situation. I hope I'll be able to get the money we owe.'

'An excellent plan. Take this copy of the bill and try very hard to persuade them to pay. I would hate anything to spoil the good feeling between us. Seriously, I don't want to make trouble for you.' I believed him. For a Soviet officer, he seemed a decent chap. We parted and I went to make preparations for my journey.

Fortunately my salary had come from Headquarters so I had money for the trip. I borrowed a travelling bag and next day I caught an early train. Just outside Tashkent we stopped unexpectedly. I alighted and went to try to discover the reason. I saw two workmen standing by the engine and I edged toward them to hear what they were saying.

'Bloody nuisance,' said one, the engine driver, I thought. 'I told them to fix it before we left.'

'How long will it take?' asked his mate.

'Couple of hours at least. I'll get started on it if you'll nip to the shop, I can see it from here over those fields. Get something to eat and some cigarettes.'

I hurried back to my compartment to get my bag which had very little in it. This was too good an opportunity to miss. 'I'll try to buy some goods for bartering and for bribes,' I thought.

I was in the shop within five minutes and was astonished to see a large range of goods. It was an Aladdin's Cave. I decided to spend as much as I could afford. Many of the items would sell well. My mouth watered when I saw three large loaves of good bread on the counter.

'What do you want?' asked the assistant.

'I want that bread, please, and some other things.'

'You can have anything you like except the bread. That's for workers only.'

'If you'll sell me the bread I'll buy enough other things for you to fulfil your norm for the day.' I knew that every shop keeper had to reach a pre-ordained target each day. His wages depended on this. He didn't hesitate but wrapped the loaves in paper and handed them over. I got them into my bag just before the engineer from the train arrived. I asked the shopkeeper for:

24 bottles of cologne
12 bottles of perfume
12 boxes of tooth powder
12 boxes of face powder
5 bottles of wine
2,500 cigarettes

He was delighted with my order and, leaning towards me, whispered, 'Would you like some fish? Some of the fish I have under the counter?' Looking round, he furtively pulled out five pickled herrings and five smoked fish. 'I'll wrap them for you.' I had great difficulty forcing everything into my bag. I settled the bill and walked back to the train as fast as my heavy load would allow.

My neighbour in the carriage was an elderly disabled man. He was amazed to see my laden bag. 'If only I could get to the shop,' he said ruefully. 'My daughter's husband is in the army and I am going to stay with her so that I can look after my grandchildren while she goes to work. I'd love to take some presents for her.'

I felt sorry for the man, looked at my watch and judged I had enough time to make another trip to the shop before the train left so I offered to go. 'What would you like me to buy for you?' I asked.

'Cologne, perfume, powder and any food or wine you can get and tobacco too if possible.' He gave me some money and a bag and said he'd look after my purchases. I ran back to the shop and managed to get most of his requirements. The shopkeeper was so pleased with my custom that he put some freshly baked fish pie into a basin and pressed me to take it.

Eventually I arrived at Polish Army Headquarters. I was overwhelmed by my welcome, for stationed there were many fellow officers I hadn't seen since before my internment, including Antek, a close friend. We even shed a few tears as we greeted each other.

I discovered that General Anders had been called to Moscow and I was forced to see his deputy, a colonel.

'I am authorised to deputise for the general in everything but financial matters,' he informed me when I told my story. 'Major P. has the responsibility for that. You'll find him in the office next door.'

'I certainly won't give you any money!' shouted Major P. when I made my request. 'I haven't got access to that sort of cash and if I had I wouldn't hand it over to you. How dare you enlist soldiers without proper authorisation?'

'I couldn't wait for authorisation. If I had, the men would have died of starvation or exposure. Some were even on the point of rioting. They would have found themselves back in a Soviet prison and the rest would have been conscripted into the Soviet Army. I took the course I thought best.'

'Then it's your funeral isn't it? I've nothing more to say to you. You'll get nothing from me.' There was no point in staying so I stormed from the room and stood still outside the door to regain my composure. 'How can I go back to Bukhara with no money? How can I break it to the troops that there will no longer be food for them?' My mind raced.

Suddenly I was struck by a truly wonderful idea – possibly the best one I'd ever had. I knocked at the colonel's office door and walked in, smiling.

'I see you've been successful in your mission,' he said. 'Well done.'

'On the contrary, sir. Not only will the major give me no money but he was extremely rude to me. Before the colonel could respond I went on. 'However, I remember receiving notification

that Stalin has offered to lend our army one hundred million roubles.'

'That is correct but...'

'I also read that our army has yet to take him up on his offer.'

'Again correct but...'

'Then, sir, I would be very grateful if your major would provide me with a letter to take back to Bukhara, stating that any monies owed, for food and heating for the barracks in Bukhara now or in the future, will be deducted from the amount of that generous loan.'

The colonel leaned back in his chair and laughed. 'You've got a nerve. You know as well as I do that we'll never get that money, promise or no promise. But there's nothing to stop us pretending that we believe it, is there? Do you think a letter from my major will do the trick with the colonel in Bukhara?'

'I'm sure it will, if you'll countersign it, please.'

'Certainly I will.'

'Not you again!' Major P. expostulated. 'I told you...' I interrupted him swiftly by asking him to write the letter. 'I won't do it! You've got a bloody cheek to come back and ask me. Get out!'

I took a deep breath to calm myself and said levelly, 'If you refuse to write this letter I will be forced to tell your colonel that you have disobeyed his order – the order of a superior officer.'

He knew he was beaten and screamed at a sergeant to write the 'bloody letter'. I soon had it in my hand, the colonel countersigned it and wished me well. I spent a happy evening with my old friends.

Back in Bukhara, I went at once to the Soviet colonel's office. Seeing my smiling face, he looked relieved.

'I see you've managed to get hold of the cash otherwise you'd look less cheerful.'

'I've brought you something better than cash,' I answered. 'And what's more it's for the full amount – for food and heating.'

'Splendid. But what can be better than cash?'

127

'This.' I placed the letter in his hand. 'Money can be stolen but this is no good to anyone but you.'

'Wonderful!' he cried, perusing the document. 'It's a pleasure doing business with you. A small drink of vodka to seal the deal?'

The next day I was in my office when Marian, one of my clerks, walked through, followed by a young woman. It was Anna who had been treated so unfairly in Farab. I saw that she recognised me but she turned away and tried to hurry past. There were things I needed to say to her so I quickly interposed myself between her and the door. 'It's Anna Grzymała Siedlecka, isn't it? Can I be of assistance to you?' I asked.

'No thank you,' in a cold even tone. 'I do not require help.'

Dratted woman! How was it that she always managed to get under my skin? Still, I did owe her an apology. 'Anna, I've hoped, for a long time that I would have the chance to apologise to you. After you had left Farab I discovered the true nature of the officer who accused you of immoral behaviour. He was, in fact, the one who was deceitful and a liar. I now know that you were innocent. Please accept my sincere apology for my treatment of you.' I felt I'd acquitted myself well with this speech – apologetic but not grovelling. I was left speechless by her haughty reply.

'I accept your apology, Captain, but I repeat, I do not need anything from you. Now, please excuse me.' And she brushed past me and was gone. Well, I'd done my best. I could do no more.

I was sorry to be posted away from Bukhara to Krasnowodsk in the spring of 1942 but I was happy in the knowledge that the people for whom I had been responsible were safe and that we knew the whereabouts of those who had been relocated. I felt sure that one day, when the war was over we would be able to contact them and that they would be free to return home.

Letters

An interpretation of an extract from a letter and a complete letter from Dziadek's friend, Antek, who worked at the Polish Army Headquarters in Jangi-Jul, near Tashkent.

25.5.42

I'm sure it will be difficult for you to leave beautiful Bukhara where I hear, from reliable sources, you are charming a beautiful young woman upon the Bukharan rugs – not a Turkoman or Uzbec but a genuine Polish one. I assume you will have to end it and that tears will fall as you depart. I know you have plenty of experience in that area, you devil!

10.10.42
Dearest Kostek,

We almost leapt around with delight when, yesterday, we saw your name on some orders which had just arrived. We have thought of you often and cried alcoholic tears! As a reward for what you have been through, you have received this important nomination. 'High Representative', don't forget your ever-loving friends!

We didn't have too bad a time. We remained in Kozielsk until the end of June, then they deported us to Griazoviec near Vologra. We left there to join the army which was already gathering. I suspect they (the Soviets) intended to deport us to work in the far north, but the negotiations (with the army) which had already begun, spoiled the glorious plans of our allies. During this time we did not work, and the quarters and food were relatively good. We have to admit that fate was kind to us.

Conditions here are difficult.

Some of the instructions you receive are my efforts. I would prefer to be doing what you do.

When I receive details of your address, I will try to forward, as soon as possible, your salary for September and October (at the moment 800 roubles per month for a captain). I will also try to send compensation for the items you have lost. This will amount to 2,000 roubles. You are now on the list of Headquarter Staff which is why you are now to receive a salary!

Let us know, briefly by telegram, what you have achieved so far and keep us informed of developments. When you have time, write and tell us all about your experiences thus far. You can send it by hand – people are always travelling between here and there and back again. If you feel very kind you could also send us something to smoke. We hear that you have access to tobacco, fruit and God knows what else. For the last ten days we have been smoking left-overs as there is nothing available here.

Keep warm, don't chase after any of the harem ladies or some Pasha will turn you into a eunuch!

Warmest regards,
Antek.

Medals and Ribbons

Dziadek in uniform with Juhas

I've been meaning to ask Dziadek about a photograph which stands on the piano. It's of him wearing his army uniform, although he is clearly far beyond the age for active service. As I am a little early for our lesson and he hasn't got a photo ready; I take the chance of bringing this one over to him. 'Will you tell me about this?' I ask. He laughs.

'People come from Poland. Make film for television from me. I say my stories and bet I get into uniform still. See,' he taps the picture, 'I right.'

'You look good in it. Did you see the television programme?'

'Yes. Video. Had to send back.'

I point to the ribbons across Dziadek's chest in the photo. 'What are these for? I ask.

'For medals.' He levers himself up from the settee and crosses to the bureau. He opens it and brings out two oblong boxes. Once re-seated he opens one of them. On a strip of velvet lie five medals. 'Allies give these,' he says. He points to each in turn: 'For fighting in war, for officer in war, for defending in war, this for Palestine intelligence and this for Italy – Ancona intelligence and Monte Cassino.' He recites the list without emotion, and I am struck by what a slice of history lies in that little box. What scenes of horror and acts of heroism it represents.

Now he's opening the second box. His face has changed, has taken on an almost tender expression. 'Poland give these,' he says. Again he points and explains, 'Long service, serving Poland, a merit medal and this…' The red cross, embellished with gold and attached to a blue and maroon ribbon bears the letters PR.

'What does PR mean?' I ask.

'Polonia Restituta,' he says as he replaces the medals and closes the lid of the box. Clearly he doesn't want to say any more about them so I thank him for explaining them to me.

I fetch an atlas and ask Dziadek to show me his wartime journey. He points it out as well as he can, although many of the places he mentions are not shown on the map.[4] 'Kleck, Vilno,

---

[4]For locations, see Glossary of names, people and places

Lithuanian prisons, finish in Minsk, Siberian labour camps, finish in Kalinos, Buzuluk, Farab, Nukus, back to Farab, Bukhara, Krasnowodsk, Guzar, Iran, Palestine, Egypt, Iraq and Italy. He jabs his finger on the town of Ancona, on the Adriatic coast. 'Here I marry. War finish.'

'What exactly was your work in the war?' I've been longing to ask this question ever since our lessons began.

'Here (pointing to Kalinos) to here (pointing to Krasnowodsk) I make safety for my peoples. Here (pointing Guzar) to here (Ancona) I ask, I listen.'

'Ask, listen?'

He shrugs. 'Intelligence.'

And there is something in his tone of voice which makes me realise that, vital as his Intelligence work must have been, it had not touched his heart in the same way as his mission to ensure the safety of his own people had done.

After the lesson I Google 'Polonia Restituta' and discover that this medal was awarded only for 'outstanding achievement in the service of Poland.'

A Mascot and Man's Best Friend

Dziadek is looking at a pen and ink drawing of a bear. One of them shows it apparently playing with some soldiers. 'My wife draw,' he explains, and then opens a book entitled *The 1989 Royal Tournament, Earls Court*. On page 202 of this official programme I see the same drawing and the words, 'Illustrated by Anna Dzierżek'.

'Oh, I understand. Your wife illustrated this article.'

'Yes.' He reads the title of the article, by W.A.Lasocki, 'Voytek – The Soldier Bear.' Voytek mascot,' he says. 'I see in Palestine. He at Monte Cassino. He at Ancona.Very clever. Help carry munitions'

The brown bear was born in Iran. When he was about three months old his mother was killed by hunters. He was rescued by locals who sold him to some Polish soldiers who happened to be passing. They fed him on diluted condensed milk and the tiny cub fell asleep, cuddled up close to one of the soldiers.

When the team reached the army camp in Palestine the officer in charge agreed that the bear could stay. He was given the name Voytek and even entered on the records of the 22nd Artillery Supply Company of the 2nd Polish Corps. The bear had become their mascot. He had joined the army.

Voytek flourished and it seemed no time before he was fully grown. He loved to wrestle and play with the soldiers. He also took baths and showers with them. One morning he went for an early bath on his own. A terrified scream ensued and, on investigation the guard found an Arab on his knees begging to be rescued from the wild beast. Voytek had disturbed one of a gang of munition thieves. He'd won his first battle and was given a bottle of beer as a reward. Apart from beer, he had one other favourite item of refreshment. Whenever they could the soldiers brought him a bunch of grapes. He would sit, happily pulling one grape off at a time, relishing the flavour and making soft, contented noises.

At Monte Cassino, in 1944, once accustomed to the sound of bursting shells, Voytek worked tirelessly to help with the unloading of large guns and heavy artillery shells for use in the battle. Afterwards the official cap badge of the 22nd Company was changed to incorporate a brown bear carrying a shell.

Voytek stayed with the 22nd Company, playing with and working alongside the servicemen, until the end of the war. The soldiers would have liked to take him back to their homeland but this was not possible, and they themselves scattered to all parts of the world. Voytek was given to Edinburgh Zoo where he became its favourite attraction, loved by all. He died at the age of 22 after an extraordinary life. He has featured in books, on radio and television and in films. There are memorial tablets to him at the British War Museum in London and at Edinburgh Zoo. There is a life-sized bronze model of Voytek and memorabilia at the Polish Institute and Sikorski Museum in London.

During my lesson with Dziadek I don't learn all this about Voytek. Danka fills me in later. Dziadek wants to move on to other animals, namely dogs. He flicks through his album. 'Can't have bear at home,' he says. 'Have plenty dogs.' He shows me Esma, who was in Italy, Żulik from Manchester, Bey and Juhas, both Londoners. It is Bey he always comes back to, though. 'He best dog. Clever – he not like police.'

One evening, Dziadek and Anna returned home to find they had been burgled. There wasn't much missing – there wasn't much to take – but the house was in a dreadful mess. The police were summoned and took details. As they were going, one of them said, 'There have been a lot of break-ins round here lately. You should get yourselves a dog.'

A few days later Dziadek and Danka were at the RSPCA kennels, faced with dogs of all breeds and of no particular breed, dogs of every shape, size and colour. Dziadek's gaze kept returning to an odd-looking ginger one.

Danka noticed. 'Dad, you can't have that,' she said. 'It's so ugly.'

'Appearances aren't everything,' he replied. 'It's got an intelligent face.'

'Mum will hate it. You know she doesn't like ginger hair. That dog's even got a ginger nose.'

'It's gazing at me. We are connecting. It likes me and I like it.' The RSPCA officer saw them looking at the ginger dog and came over. 'That's a lovely fellow,' he said. 'He's an Alsatian crossed with Labrador. He was supposed to be a police dog but in training sessions instead of getting hold of the burglar, he caught up with him and then rolled over to be tickled.'

'Not much use to you then,' Danka remarked. 'You want a dog that will catch the burglars, don't you?'

'He's big and looks fierce, that's what matters. I'll take him.'

Anna wasn't impressed with the new dog but admitted that, although he was ugly, he looked noble. 'Why don't you call him Bey?' she suggested. So Bey he became. ('Bey' was the second part of the name of each of the Turkish noblemen who fought in the Battle of Vienna).[5]

A few days later there was a ring on the door bell. Bey, who by now knew that it was his job to guard the house and all who lived there, made a dreadful racket. Dziadek held his collar firmly and answered the door. Two policemen stood outside.

'We've come to check that all is well with your new dog,' they said. 'We're the dog handlers who were training him. We always check on dogs after they've been re-homed.'

Bey seemed to relax once the policemen were seated on the settee drinking tea. They petted him and professed themselves satisfied that he'd found a good home. Thanking Dziadek for his hospitality, they rose to go and made as if to shake hands with him. Bey suddenly flew at them, snarling. Possibly he thought their extended hands were some sort of threat. Before Dziadek realised what was happening the dog had the two men pinned up against the wall. In a sharp tone Dziadek called, 'Bey, down! Bey!' Reluctantly Bey released the policemen who fortunately took it in good part.

'We could do with you at the dog training centre,' one of them said as they left.

Dziadek took Bey for his last walk of the day at the same time each evening. The dog quickly learned to recognise the theme tune of *The Bill*. He merely cocked an ear at the start of the programme and at advert breaks, but when the final music played

---

[5]Battle of Vienna took place on 14th July 1683

he fetched his lead from the kitchen and stood expectantly in front of his master.

One day, as Anna and Dziadek walked to the town together, Anna was amazed at how many people, mainly older women, greeted her husband. 'How do you know them all?' she asked.

'I not only know them to speak to,' replied Dziadek, 'but I know a lot about them. That lady over there has just had a hysterectomy. The first one I spoke to has bunions and the tall one outside Boots is just back from her daughter's wedding in Canada.'

'How on earth do you know all that? You don't speak enough English to have proper conversations.'

'Easy. When you have a dog everyone else with a dog wants to talk to you. I don't have to say very much – just "Good day." All these ladies just stop and tell me all these things. I don't understand everything they say but I only have to smile and nod.'

It's no wonder that people recognised Dziadek, even without his dog. He was distinctive in his trench coat, black beret, worn at a jaunty angle and swinging his walking stick. Bey loved to walk to town with him. His favourite place was the pet stall at the market. After being greeted by the stall-holder he would sniff along the boxes ranged at the front and with his teeth pick out whichever dog-chew he fancied. Dziadek would pay for it and anything else he wanted, and then he and Bey would head for home. The favoured chew wouldn't be eaten until home was reached but, as Dziadek explains to me with actions, 'Bey has big chew, stick out like this. He not eat, but he has water from mouth. Drip, drip.'

Suddenly, in my mind's eye I see Dziadek's big ginger dog. He is bearing a handlebar chew from which hang long threads of drool which swing backwards and forwards as the two firm friends slowly make their way home together.

Anna

*Anna and Dziadek soon after their wedding in Italy –
with Esma*

Objects, rather than photographs are the focus of today's lesson. Dziadek has lined up three on the coffee table – a large glass plate, richly decorated with silver twelve-legged creatures on a green background, a blue and silver glass cocktail set, and a small blue and green Murano glass vase. He touches each lovingly. 'Honeymoon,' he says. 'We buy on honeymoon. Married Ancona, Italy, 1946.'

The items are understandably of great sentimental value to him, but when I think about them later, something else occurs to me. Apart from the three 'treasures' restored to him by his sister, Ania after the war, Dziadek has nothing at all from his family life in Poland. He has no heirlooms, no record of family history. All exiles, forced to flee from their homelands are in the same position. He, and they, must start again with a new set of 'heirlooms'. Thus, the objects which adorn the coffee table are of extra significance.

To return to the lesson, 'We live in Bishop's Palace. Ancona,' he says. 'Beautiful house. Rosa Capone, she keep house. Cook. Clean.'

I write down what he tells me about the house and housekeeper but, in truth, I am more interested to understand how Dziadek and Anna came to be married at all. In her memoirs Anna wrote of Dziadek,
'I learned to respect him but could not warm to him'. What happened to bring about such a change in her feelings between 1942 (when her memoir ends) and 1946?

From conversations I had with Anna before she died, and from what I've learned from Danka, other members of the family and old friends, I try to put together the Dziadek/Anna story. Dziadek also drops some remarks on the subject during lessons – a few more pieces to the jigsaw.

After the first few unfortunate meetings, Anna finds herself working in SK11, the Intelligence Corps in Guzar, where Dziadek was one of the commanders. They met next in Egypt. There, Dziadek, who was working in counter-intelligence, persuaded Anna to work as his secretary, a sought-after post. He felt he owed her the job, having been unfair when she appealed to him about her former dismissal. By then she was a sergeant. He found her quick and intelligent, and he never regretted the appointment. In fact, when he was transferred to Ancona, with some of his office staff, Anna was one of the NCOs he took with him.

By now, he found himself attracted to this beautiful, popular young woman. At first she gave him no encouragement. He was some twenty years older than she was, and he had the reputation of being a 'ladies' man'. Dziadek wouldn't give up, however. Perhaps he found it hard to accept rejection after his many conquests. Then he discovered that he was in a position to help Anna. He heard that she was desperate to track down her brother, Bohdan, who she thought had been in a German prisoner of war camp. Using his contacts, and through the services of the Red Cross, Dziadek discovered that he was still in Germany, after having been interred in Murnau Camp. The Red Cross facilitated Bohdan's journey from there to Ancona, where he and Anna were reunited.

It seems that gratitude and Dziadek's persistence paid off, for finally, in 1946 the couple were married. Antek, a friend of Dziadek's from before the war, and who had kept in touch with him throughout, was the best man.

After the marriage things did not go altogether smoothly. Anna took up residence in the Bishop's Palace with her new husband, but this did not suit housekeeper Rosa Capone. Dziadek was a favourite of hers. She had loved to cook him large Italian meals. She had indulged his passion for bridge by catering lavishly for late night bridge parties. She didn't want to relinquish her duties to the new wife, and fierce arguments ensued. Rosa had even arranged for a tailor to make a couple of suits for Dziadek.

Danka showed me one of them that he'd kept – for fifty years. It was black, pinstriped with big lapels. 'He would never throw it away,' she said, 'although mum wouldn't let him wear it. She said it made him look like a gangster.'

Life cannot have been easy for Dziadek in that palace, torn as he was between two strong-minded women. Perhaps a sense of relief was mixed with the sadness he felt when Anna had to leave Ancona for England at the end of 1946, prior to the birth of her baby.

Everything was arranged for the baby to be born at Penley Polish Hospital in Wrexham, North Wales. Anna was to be met at Victoria railway station and taken there by a nurse. Unfortunately, she went into labour on Calais station as she was alighting from the boat train. She was taken to the local military hospital where Danka was born. All necessities for the baby had been sent ahead to Penley, so nurses cut up towels for nappies and a sheet and blanket to wrap her in. After a few days Anna and Danka were put on the ferry for Dover, where they boarded the train bound for Victoria. When they arrived, there was no-one to meet them. Feeling sure someone would come soon Anna sat, first on the station and later in the waiting room where at least there was a coal fire. She was still sitting there at 11pm when the stationmaster made his last round. Anna explained what had happened.

'Someone from the hospital will come tomorrow, I'm sure,' she said.

'You can't sit here all night. Come and use my room. I'll make you a warm drink and then give you some privacy.' He helped her with a trunk she had with her. It contained Dziadek's clothes which were to be stored at the hospital until he finished his work in Ancona, when he would come to England. Then the kind man gave her warm milk and shared his sandwiches before he left. She fed and changed Danka and eventually fell asleep.

The next day Anna sat, once more, in the waiting room, but by nightfall she knew that she couldn't impose on the stationmaster for another day. Also, she was concerned about Danka and was, herself, cold and exhausted.

'If someone doesn't come tomorrow,' she said to the stationmaster, 'I'll leave the trunk with you, if I may, and I'll try to get in touch with the Polish Consulate.' Once more she shared his sandwiches and spent the night in his office.

Unable to sleep, Anna was up before dawn. It was then she remembered a remark of Dziadek's a couple of weeks previously. Referring to his brother-in-law, he had said, 'Alex is doing well for himself. He's working in London and staying at the Rembrandt Hotel.'

'Why didn't I think of Alex sooner?' Anna thought. I'll ask the stationmaster to help me to get in touch with him.' She gave up all hope of sleep and, as Danka was fretful, she went into the station concourse and began to walk up and down with the baby. Suddenly she heard Polish voices. Two Polish airmen were standing nearby, looking at a timetable.

'Pomozcie mnie!' ('Help me please!') she called. Astonished, they looked up and hurried to her side. She explained her predicament.

'Never fear, madam,' they said. 'We will find this Rembrandt Hotel and bring the gentleman to you.' One of them wrote down Alex's name; they kissed her hand and departed.

Two hours later Alex was on the scene, handsome, dashing. 'Like a knight in shining armour,' is how Anna described him later. He sorted everything out, thanked the soldiers and the stationmaster, bought Anna a hot meal and found transport. He travelled to Wrexham with her and Danka, and ensured they were properly settled into the hospital. Finally he contacted Dziadek and told him the whole story.

Two weeks later Dziadek left Ancona and met his daughter for the first time. By the end of1946 the family was in residence at a re-settlement camp in Cheshire.

A Camp and a Batman

Delamere Park Resettlement Camp.

Dziadek has two photographs ready for me today. I bend over the first. It's the entrance of what looks like a country estate with a drive sweeping away into the distance. I can make out the words 'Delamere Park Camp' on a sign above the gate. On one of the gate posts a notice reads,

POLSKI 0802

DELAMERE

'This camp,' Dziadek explains, 'many Polish soldiers come there for re-settle.' I know he was Commandant at Delamere,

145

responsible for re-settling hundreds of ex-servicemen both in Britain and overseas. 'I learn make handbags,' he adds.

'You made handbags?' It seems such an unlikely story that I think I've misheard.

'Yes, and belts and briefcase.'

'Why?'

'To make money when leave camp.' Then, with a rueful smile and a shrug, 'No money.'

At the end of the war the MOD didn't know what to do with the many Polish servicemen who ended up on British soil. These men and women had fought alongside the Allies against the Nazis, not just for their own freedom but for the freedom of Western Europe. Now they were disillusioned and bitter about the outcome of the Yalta Conference[6], in 1945.

The agreement which was reached not only denied Poland independence, but handed the country over to Soviet Russia – handed it over to the very regime that had orchestrated the invasion from the east in 1939 – to the regime which was responsible for the torture and slaughter of thousands of Poles.

Clearly the British Government could not ignore this uncomfortable truth. It must do its best to accommodate, train and re-settle as many Poles as possible. To this end, a number of re-settlement camps were set up around the country. Delamere Park, previously an American base, was one of them.

At the end of 1946, General Anders' Command Group arrived from Italy, under the supervision of Lieutenant Colonel Dzierżek – Dziadek.

He's still looking at the photograph and says, 'Live in huts, beczka smiechu.'

---

[6] See *Appendix 2*

'Barrel of laughs,' translates Danka. 'That's what they called them. They were those round-topped Nissen huts – you know, a bit like barrels.'

'What were they like inside?' I ask Dziadek. 'What furniture did you have?'

'Beds, chest, cupboard, chairs to fold up, table.'

'How many rooms?'

'One big. Blanket hang make bedroom.'

'What about a cooker?'

'Later cooker. First eat in mess. Big cookhouse.'

Eventually, after the arrival of cast-iron stoves, families were issued with ration books and could buy food and cook independently. Men were offered training to enable them to earn a living once they moved from the camp. Dziadek's training was in leather work which explains the allusion to handbags.

Delamere seems to have been the place where reality hit home. The cruel reality that there may never be a home-going, that the camaraderie of army days was gone, and that as the men donned their grey demob suits their very Polishness seemed to be disappearing.

Wisniewski, the child-minding batman.

'Who's this?' I ask looking at the second photograph Dziadek has selected. It's of a man turned towards a child. 'It's not you with Danka, is it?' Dziadek laughed.

'No me, Wisniewski.'

'A friend of yours?'

A pause and then, 'Not really friend. He work me.'

'Batman,' says Danka. 'Wisniewski was your batman.'

'Ah, Wisniewski batman and look after baby.'

When Dziadek was the Commander of the camp in Ancona, Italy, he was already responsible for the movement of Polish troops to a variety of countries for re-settlement. One evening another officer approached him with a problem.

'In the guardroom we have a Silesian peasant,' he said. 'As usual he's dead drunk. He's been involved in drunken brawls more times than I can remember. Nothing anyone says has any effect on him. He's illiterate and has lost touch with his wife and family, so he's got nothing to lose. We simply don't know what to do with him. We can't recommend him for re-settlement. Prison seems the only option. What shall we do?'

Dziadek thought for a moment then, 'I'll see him tomorrow when he's sobered up. I'll see what I can do.'

No-one knows exactly what Dziadek said to the man when he went to the little cell the next day. 'Straight talk,' is how he described it to Anna. At the end of it he had elicited a promise of reform and teetotalism in return for an offer of employment as batman.

'This is your very last chance,' he warned. 'If there is even one report of your drinking alcohol or of fighting you will go to prison.'

Dziadek seemed to have inspired respect and gratitude in Wisniewski for he became the model batman: loyal, hardworking and devoted to his Officer. For a year he maintained the exemplary behaviour. Towards the end of 1946, when news arrived that Anna had given birth to a baby girl, Wisniewski promptly disappeared. He was found a day later, very drunk. He was in the town, sitting at the side of the street, singing loudly. He was marched back to the guardroom and Dziadek was summoned.

'I warned you,' he said, deeply disappointed. 'No more chances. You no longer work for me. I shall recommend that you serve a prison sentence.'

Wisniewski opened his eyes wide and then, staggering across the room towards him, he burst into tears. 'But sir,' he sobbed 'we have had a baby. We have had a baby!'

'What I say?' Dziadek looks at me appealingly at this point in the story. 'I say nothing. I do nothing. He stay batman. He never do again.'

When the Ancona office closed, Dziadek brought Wisniewski to Delamere Park. It was then that the batman's duties were extended to include looking after the baby. He was little Danka's almost constant companion until she was five years old. He always referred to her as 'the child', and was fiercely protective. One day, as Dziadek walked home from his office, he saw smoke rising from behind the trees which lined the path. On investigation he found Wisniewski burning newspaper. Over the fire he waved a pair of long underpants while he chanted strange words. 'What on earth are you doing?' cried Dziadek. 'Put that fire out. You could have the whole forest alight.'

'Never fear sir,' was the reply. 'This is Silesian magic. I am making sure no-one will ever harm the child.' If ever an unknown person approached Danka the batman would quickly interpose himself between her and the stranger. 'No-one is allowed to look straight at the child before first looking into my eyes,' he said. 'You can never be sure who might give her the evil eye.'

After five years, Delamere Camp closed. Broken-hearted, Wisniewski begged to be allowed to stay with the family when it moved to Manchester, but money was very short and work not easy to find. The batman insisted he would work for nothing but Dziadek simply could not afford to feed another mouth. He arranged for Wisniewski to go to a training camp prior to settling in France.

He saw him once more. 'He come for making chicken house for child,' he tells me.

Wisniewski had turned up to say 'Farewell' and while he was there he had converted the Anderson shelter into a chicken house and erected a run.

'Eggs are good for the child,' he said. 'I hope she will enjoy them.' Then he left and went out of their lives for ever.

'He good batman,' concludes Dziadek. 'I hope he OK.'

The House on the Corner

The House on the Corner

Dziadek shows me a picture of a house. It's large, Edwardian and almost obscured by trees.

'My house,' he says. 'Corner house. St Mary's Road, Manchester.'

As I look at the photograph I remember an occasion, a couple of years ago, when Anna told me all about the family's relocation to Manchester.

When the last soldier to be re-settled had left the camp in Delamere, Dziadek's work there was done and he needed to find a home for himself and his family.

'In Manchester,' he said.

'Why not London?' asked Anna. 'I'd rather live in London.'

'Lots of people from Delamere have gone to Manchester so we'll have connections there. Also that's where Uncle Jan[7] wants to open his medical practice. He says he's got contacts in Manchester – other doctors who will help him get started. We can't afford to buy a house on our own and he's keen to come in with us.'

'There are lots of Polish people in London too.'

'But we won't know so many of them. And anyway, Uncle Jan wants to practice in Manchester. We'll be able to afford a bigger house there than we could in London. I've heard property is very expensive there. In Manchester we'll get a house big enough for you, me, Danka and Uncle Jan to live in *and* with enough space for him to have a consulting room.

And that was the end of the discussion.

On the next Saturday, Dziadek and his uncle took a day trip by train to Manchester. They entered the first estate agents they came to. What follows is what they told Anna on their return. They managed to make the young man behind the counter

---

[7]*Jan was the brother of Maria and of Alexander Borowski, with whom Dziadek had stayed in Warsaw when he first arrived in Poland from Soviet Russia.*

understand that they were looking for a large house. He handed them a file full of properties for sale. They sat down and proceeded to study it. They would have to take out a mortgage and had calculated how much they could afford. Unfortunately most of the larger houses were well above that amount. Then they came across the house on the corner of St Mary's Road. The young man, noticing they were discussing it, came over and, using mimes, drawings and their Polish dictionary explained what the property entailed.

'I think he means it's got four floors and lots of rooms,' said Dziadek.

'And cellars. Good for storage,' added Dr Borowski.

'It's got trees all round it. It will be like living in a country house.' Perhaps Dziadek had visions of his Uncle Edward's mansion.

'Look at the plan,' enthused the Doctor. 'This room will make a perfect consulting room and there's plenty of space for people to wait just here. This is certainly the house for us.'

'It is.' Dziadek turned to the estate agent. 'We have this one please.' Each of them pulled a wad of banknotes from their pockets. 'How much now?'

'Don't you want to see the house?' asked the bemused young man.

'No, we just pay,' they insisted. The agent fetched papers for them to sign and they gave him a contact address and counted out the deposit. There wasn't much left over at the end. Then, triumphantly carrying a smudgy black and white picture of the corner house, the two men returned to Delamere to give Anna the good news.

'The day we moved in was the first time we saw it,' Anna told me. 'It was a bleak, rainy day in winter. The house looked forbidding, tall with bricks of battleship grey. Straight away I could see that, in summer, the trees would keep out most of the light. If my heart sank when I looked at the outside, it hit the ground when I stepped inside the front door. A smell of musty damp hit me. The large hallway was dark. The electric light wouldn't work and it was absolutely freezing. Paint was flaking and wallpaper peeling everywhere in the house. There were huge gas brackets fixed in all of the rooms, but above all I was conscious of the seeping damp and cold.

While I tried to light a fire in the drawing room, the men ran from room to room in delight.

"It's bigger than I thought it would be. We might even be able to take in lodgers." I heard Jan Borowski shout. Danka was already filthy from rolling on the floor, and when at last I did manage to light the fire, the room filled with smoke. Even later, after we'd had the chimney swept and had a fire in the grate, the drawing room was never warm. Most of the heat seemed to go up the chimney and, although you could roast a bit of yourself if you were up very close to the fire, the water in the flower vase at the other end of the room would freeze. The electrics were very temperamental too. When they decided to work they would flicker or go off suddenly. The whole place was a nightmare. Looking back, I don't know how I stuck it.'

The one gleam in this otherwise dismal picture was the close proximity of the 'connections' Dziadek had been so optimistic about when choosing Manchester over London. He contacted some of 'his' men, who were only too pleased to give a hand with repairs and redecoration. As time went on the house on the corner became an unofficial citizens' advice bureau for the local Polish community. Dziadek's men came to ask his advice on everything from setting up in business to which girl to marry. He acted as best man at numerous weddings and was godfather to many babies. He was a facilitator, the centre of a network. In exchange for all he did for them his men were always ready to help him in any way they could.

Dziadek was respected and loved by many Polish people throughout Britain and further afield. He had helped to bring thousands to safety. He had commanded and fought alongside many more and he had worked hard to ensure that those who were unable to return to Poland were satisfactorily re-settled.

'We were never allowed to pay for a meal in the Polish restaurant,' Anna said. 'And we received invitations to all sorts of functions from all over the world.

The men my husband had commanded in the war used to come and thank him for what he'd done for them. When we lived in St Mary's Road, and there was an important function at the Polish Club, three Daimlers would draw up at our door, one for each of us. They were driven by his men. Many of them were doing very well. They'd become plumbers, electricians, builders and even entrepreneurs. Gradually they'd bought nice houses and prestigious cars. Once, one of the Daimler drivers said to me, "It's clear that your husband's an officer. He hasn't got a car." He was right. We could never afford a car and it was the same with many of the other officers, even the generals.'

Meanwhile, the house on the corner had to be furnished.

'All we brought with us from the camp were our army chests of clothes, three knives, forks and spoons, one pan and ladle, three camp beds, and some 'utility' sheets, blankets and towels along with a few bits and pieces we'd managed to buy while we were at Delamere. I found out about house clearance sales and sent the two men off to see what they could buy. The first time, they bought three beds very cheaply, and after that they went to every sale they could. I never went with them so I don't know how they managed with the bidding as neither of them could speak much English. It's a good job our house was large as most of the furniture they bought was massive. I think it was from houses of former mill owners and the like, so it was of good quality. Over time they bought huge dressing tables, wardrobes, more beds, a dining room suite, couches, armchairs, bookshelves, pots and pans, cutlery, linen and even a piano – everything we could possibly need. Their favourite buys were boxes of 'bits' – unspecified, and job lots of books.

They also discovered 'Henrys', a shop full of cheap, fire-salvaged goods. 'Eventually we had lino, carpets and rugs, even if they did all smell somewhat scorched.'

Anna was telling me all this in the Tooting house. I caught myself looking round the small dining room of their modest semi.

She laughed. 'Yes, this is some of the furniture we brought from St. Mary's Road. We had to get rid of a lot, but Kostek wouldn't hear of parting with this. You can hardly move in here. I know, but we're used to it and we like it. This dining table has seen many battles, I can tell you.'

'Battles?'

'Yes. Whenever we had a dinner party for our ex-service friends, the men would re-enact the battles in which they'd been involved. The pepper pot would be the enemy. The salt, the Allies. Cutlery would be pressed into use too, to show lines of defence or attack. They could always suggest improvements on what had actually happened. They won so many battles on this table. Sometimes they'd argue about different strategies almost all night. I'd go to bed and leave them to it.'

Soon the house on the corner was filling up with people as well as furniture. First came Jan Borowski's son, daughter-in-law and daughters along with another doctor and his family. Then, two single men.

'I spent all my time skivvying.' Anna said. 'I did most of the cooking and all the cleaning, but when Jan Borowski died and his son's family moved away I decided enough was enough. My husband wanted to advertise for more lodgers.

"We need the money to help with the mortgage," he said. I knew that was true. The house was a black hole as far as money was concerned.

"If we have more lodgers, they'll have to cook and clean for themselves," I told him. "I've been offered a place at the Manchester Art College and I start in September when Danka begins school." I'd always wanted to train as an artist. I would have gone to Warsaw Art Academy if the war hadn't happened. I knew this was my chance and that I'd regret it for ever if I didn't take it.

'So Danka started school and I started college. Other members of the family and friends came as lodgers through the years, but they looked after themselves and were not my responsibility. My husband continued to work at the Dunlop Factory. It was hard and unpleasant work. Then he became very ill with pneumonia.' Anna paused for a moment in her story then said, 'When he recovered, the Doctor said he couldn't go back to the heavy work at Dunlop's so he tried some hare-brained money-making schemes of his own. Needless to say, I was always dragged into them, but none of them made a penny.'

Anna told me that first, Dziadek and his friend, Mr Bagaj, decided to cash in on a secret recipe for pickled herrings; a recipe which had been in Anna's family for generations. They persuaded her to make a vast quantity and, in the cellar, they put it in the jars they'd previously collected and washed. Then they bought some vodka and set out to visit all the continental grocery stores in Manchester and even as far afield as Bury.

'In each shop they'd give a sample jar to the owner and drink some vodka with him,' Anna said. 'Everyone said how delicious the herrings were and that they'd think about placing an order, but nobody ever did. Each evening Bagaj and my husband would reel home, very happy but penniless. That "business" came to an end pretty soon'.

The next thing they tried was leatherwork. After all, as Dziadek said to Anna, 'This is the skill I learned so that I could earn my living. Now is the time to put this knowledge to good use.' He bought, very cheaply, a huge, ancient leather press and cutter. (He moved this machine to London with him years later. It was still in his garden shed when he went to live with Danka in Cheshire, and she had to pay someone to take it away.)

The leather workshop was in the cellar too. There, Dziadek and Mr Bagaj cut out jackets, belts and handbags and machine-stitched them. Then Anna was prevailed upon to add decoration, and the goods were ready for sale.

'They bought the inevitable vodka – to "oil the wheels" they said,' Anna reminisced. 'They tramped round all the markets and clothes shops but sold almost nothing. What they did sell didn't make enough profit to cover costs. So, finally, they finished the vodka and Danka and I came in for a couple of lovely suede handbags and jackets each. And that was that.'

I thought then, how strange it was that Dziadek could advise others on setting up businesses, which turned out to be successful, but could never quite manage his own. He, who had been a leader of men, had no useful skills to sell in Britain.

In Manchester, Dziadek's working life was strictly Monday to Friday. On Friday evenings a transformation took place. He bathed, cast aside his dirty working garb, sloughed off all vestiges of his 'British life' and became a Polish officer and gentleman. He donned either his regimental blazer or a suit and immersed himself in a huge variety of Polish activities. 'Even his body language altered on a Friday evening,' Danka told me.

Dziadek was instrumental in raising money to build and maintain a Polish Club, church, priest's house, and to pay the priest's salary. Every Sunday saw him collecting money for these projects and for the Saturday school where Polish children went to learn Polish history, geography, literature, music and dance. He also helped to set up Polish Scout and Guide troops, fund raising for these, as well, and involving himself in the purchase of huts in the grounds of the Polish Home at 'Penrhos', near Pwllheli on the Lleyn Peninsula, North Wales. He spent some weekends there, helping senior Guides and Scouts to convert them into an excellent centre for summer camps. The centre is still in use.

Sometimes Dziadek used Penrhos Home grounds for training his men in Pogon, a paramilitary organisation. Being Commander of this 'army' was his favourite peace-time occupation. Military manoeuvres accounted for many of his weekends.

'Mum said he just loved playing soldiers,' Danka told me.

Actually, there was a serious purpose behind Pogon. It was originally set up in the hope that a reconstituted Polish army would return home to overcome the Soviets and reclaim Poland. It continued, however, even when it was obvious that there would be no such return. This was so that the survival skills that Dziadek and other veterans had learned in the war, at a huge cost, could be passed on to the next generation.

Although he took pride in his community activities and in the achievements of the men and women whose lives had once been his responsibility, Dziadek never recovered from the bitter disappointment of being unable to return to Poland. Even after the fall of the Berlin wall, he could not return for it was not *his* Poland any more.

He was a highly intelligent and resourceful man, driven by duty and patriotism, but both he and his beloved homeland were irrevocably changed by world events.

Dziadek remained, for ever, a stranger in a foreign land.

Postscript

Konstanty Władysław Nieczuja Dzierżek – *Dziadek* – died, at the age of 97, in March 1998.

He died in the hospital which is part of a Polish sheltered housing community at Penrhos. This community is situated right next to the very centre that he had once helped Polish Scouts and Guides to acquire. It is in the grounds over which he had led his men, in Pogoń, on military manoeuvres so long ago.

He died surrounded by Polish people, cared for by Polish nurses and hearing, at the last, Polish voices.

After Dziadek's death I saw his death certificate. Under 'Former occupation' the words 'manual worker' were written. As I stared at them, there flashed through my mind the ingenuity, the courage, the blatant daring he had displayed while fighting, in a variety of ways, for his people. Suddenly I felt a sense of deep gratitude that I had met this man and was able to tell, at least in part, his remarkable story.

Joy Mawby

Appendix 1

1920
The Russo – Polish War

January – April The Bolsheviks, having taken up occupation in a large part of the Ukraine, rally forces in order to invade Poland.

Marshall Pilsudski, Commander of the Polish Army, signs an alliance with the Ukrainians. The Polish Army marches into Kiev to help with the defence of the city.

5th June The Red Army attacks, from the north. Polish and Ukrainian Armies flee.

4th July The Bolsheviks launch another offensive. The Red Army marches towards Poland. Lenin proclaims the end of bourgeois rule. Bolshevik agitators are sent among Polish people to stir up dissent.

12th July The Red Army reaches the defences around Warsaw. At this stage, news of Warsaw's overthrow is announced.

August Newspapers all over the World report Warsaw as being in Bolshevik hands.

15th August Pilsudski leads the Polish Army in a successful but dangerous and daring flank attack. Almost all of the Red Army, in the area, is wiped out.

23rd September This victory is followed up by another on the Neimen River. The Red Army collapses. Warsaw remains free.

Appendix 2

The lead-up to the Yalta Conference and beyond

In November 1943, the Heads of State of Britain, USA and Soviet Russia met to discuss the post-war future of Europe. No representative from the Polish Government in Exile was invited to the Summit. This was in spite of the fact that the issue of Poland's eastern border was to be discussed and the exiled Government had been recognised, by America and Britain, as the official governing body of Poland.

At the Conference, it was agreed that Europe would be divided into two areas or 'zones'. The western and southern territory would come under Anglo-American control. The east, which included Poland, would be the Soviet prize. Stalin stipulated that the Soviet-Polish border should follow the 'Curzon Line.' This was a line which had been originally suggested by Lord Curzon, a British Foreign Secretary, as long ago as 1920. It also nearly matched the boundary agreed in a German-Soviet Pact of 1939 (the Molotov-Ribbentrop Agreement). The Line placed about 70,000 square miles of Polish territory, including rich oil fields, inside the Soviet Union. No formal agreement was signed by the three Allies at this time.

It was at the Yalta Summit, in February 1945, that the 'Curzon Line' was confirmed as the official boundary between Soviet Russia and Poland. Again, there were no Polish Government in Exile representatives present. Nor were there in August 1945, when the next Allied Summit was held. By this time, in fact, the Allies no longer recognised the 'Exiles' as representing Poland. Stalin brought a Polish Communist Delegation to this conference at Potsdam. Here the western border of Poland was agreed. A promise was also made that 'free and unfettered elections' would be held in Poland.

In parallel with the three Allied Summits Stalin, not satisfied with the extra territory he had gained, was working steadily towards the imposition of a Soviet-style government in what remained of Poland.

In July 1944, regardless of the wishes of the indigenous population, the Communist controlled 'Polish Committee of National Liberation' was set up in Warsaw as a temporary governing body. In December, it changed its name to 'The Provisional Government of the Polish Republic' (RTRP). To Stalin's chagrin, Britain and the USA refused to recognise it as the official government of Poland. They declared that the Polish Government in Exile, comprising the remnants of the pre-war Government and operating from London, had this role.

In January 1945, the Red Army marched into Warsaw, now in ruins. The whole of Poland was soon in Soviet hands and in June 1945, the RTRP merged with The Polish Peasant Movement. One member of that Movement, Stanislaw Mikołajczyk, who was also a member of the Polish Government in Exile, returned to Poland to join the governing body, re-named The Provisional Government of National Unity (TRJN). At last, Britain and the USA agreed to recognise this body as the official Polish Government. This may have been because of the inclusion of the one member of the exiled government. It may have been because the Allies had enormous problems of their own and felt they could spend no more time negotiating on the behalf of Poles – or perhaps it was a combination. Whatever the reason, it left the millions[8] of exiled Poles without a government and removed their last chance of returning to a homeland which resembled, in any way, the one they had fought so hard to save. In one fell swoop, they had lost government and country.

---

[8] At this time there were more Poles living outside than inside Poland.

The TRJN remained in power until January 1947. A month later, elections were held. These were neither 'free' nor 'unfettered', but Britain and USA were powerless to do more than protest.

It was now that the true implications of the concessions made to Stalin at Tehran, Yalta and Potsdam became clear. The new government, backed by the might of Soviet Russia and led by Josef Cyrankiewicz, slowly but surely transformed itself into a repressive one-party replica of the one in Moscow. Stalin's plans for Poland had come to fruition.

Poland after Yalta

.... *Curzon Line*

\ \ \ \ \ \ \ \ \ *Annexed by Soviet Union 1945*

Glossary of Names, People and Places

The names of the countries to which towns and areas are ascribed in this book are current. This is to make it easier for readers to place them. During the course of history, borders have changed and countries have been re-named. The prisons and camps in which Dziadek was incarcerated and also his war time military postings, until he reached Iran, all lay within the territory then occupied by the U.S.S.R.

Konstanty Władysław Dzierżek – *Dziadek's full name*
Anna – *his wife*
Danka – *his daughter*
Maria – *his mother*
Henry – *his brother*
Ania and Irka – *his sisters*

Mr Bagaj – *Ukranian friend in Manchester*

Adam, Tadek, Stefan – *Polish friends in Railway Workers' Union*

Twer – *town, north- west of Moscow, in Soviet Russia, in which Provincial Office was situated*

Rżew – *town, in Province of Twer, in which he and family resided until May 1924*

Janek – *Polish boy smuggled over Russian-Polish border*

Kostek – *diminutive of Konstanty*

Stolcow – *town situated on Polish side of Soviet-Polish border*

Alexander Borowski – *Maria's brother, living in Warsaw*

Chadorowski, Borek – *students lodging in Alexander Borowski's house in the forest*

Krupski family – *family friends with a country house*

Tala – *beautiful daughter of Mr and Mrs Krupski*

Uncle Edward –*father's brother*

Palac w Michalowcach – *country manor house, owned by Uncle Edward, situated at Michalowce, in Poland*

'Dzierżkowice' – *name of the manor*

Mietek Alexander Szmajke – *brother-in-law*

Suwalki – *first posting after graduation from Officer Academy. In north- east Poland.*

Kleck – *second posting. Polish town bordering Soviet held territory. Now in Minsk Province of Belarus*

Vilno – *third posting. The Lithuanian capital city*

Gdansk – *Polish port on Baltic Sea. Renamed Danzig by occupying Nazis*

Kulatuwa, Wilkowiszki, Kalwaria, Kozielsk, Minsk – *Soviet prisons*

Minsk – *capital of Belarus*

Kalinos – *Soviet forced labour camp.*

Olek – *friend in prison*

Buzuluk – *Russian town where it was thought that the Polish Army was assembling*

Kolatz – *railway station which was the first stop on his journey to find the Polish Army*

Captain May – *second-in-command on the long train journey*

Tashkent – *capital of Uzbekistan*

Amu Dar'ya – *main river of Uzbekistan. It runs between the ports of Farab and Nukus*

Jagielski – *A lieutenant and a friend*

Lvov also known as Lviv – *City, formerly in Eastern Poland, later annexed by Soviets. Now largest city in western Ukraine*

Karakalpakia – *area in Amu Dar'yaDelta , at the western end of the Aral Basin*

Stanislav Świêtlik – a *captain in Polish Police Force*

Dzhizak – *town in Uzbekistan, round which there were a number of collective farms*

Jangi-Jul – *headquarters of Polish Army. Town in Uzbekistan, in region of Tashkent.*

Anna Grzymała Siedlecka – *Anna's full name*

Czardzou –*NKVD headquarters on left bank ofAmu' Darya river. In Turkmenistan*

Bukhara – *posted there after his posting in Farab. Ancient city in Uzbekistan*

Chairman Schmidt – *Chairman in charge of area in which Farab transit camp was situated*

Mr Młodzianowski – *civilian representative of Polish Government in Bukhara*

Krasnowodsk – *posted there after his posting in Bukhara. In Kazakhstan*

Antek – *friend since pre-war days. Best man at wedding. Danka's godfather.*

Griazoviec – *Soviet labour camp*

Guzar – *posted here. It was Polish Intelligence Corps Headquarters for a time.*

Voytek – *the 'Soldier Bear'. Mascot of 22nd Artillery Supply Company of 2nd Polish Corps*

Esma – *the Italian dog*

Żulik – *the Manchester dog*

Bey and Juhas – *London dogs*

Ancona, Italy – *final posting before coming to Britain. Where Anna and he were married*

Rosa Capone – *his housekeeper in Ancona*

Bohdan – *Anna's brother*

Delamere Camp – *re-settlement camp in Cheshire*

Wisniewski – *his batman*

Dr. Jan Borowski – *Maria's second brother who was joint owner of the house on the corner of St Mary's Road, Manchester*

Stanislaw Mikołajczyk – *member of Peasant Movement. Joined*

Provisional Government of National Unity, in Warsaw, in 1945

Josef Cyrankiewicz – *leader of Soviet controlled Polish*

Government, elected in February 1947

Bibliography

Davies, Norman. *Heart of Europe* (Oxford: Oxford University Press, 1984).

Koskodan, Kenneth K. *No Greater Ally* (Oxford: Osprey Publishing, 2009).

Morgan, Geoffrey. & Lasocki, W.A. *Soldier Bear* (London: Gryf Publications Ltd, 1970).

Rees, Laurence. *Behind Closed Doors* (London: Ebury Publishing, 2008).

Young, Peter. (Ed) *Battles and Campaigns* (London: Orbis Publishing, 1973).

Zamoyski, Adam. *The Polish Way* (London: John Murray (Publishers) Ltd 1987).

Websites

Aleksei Jordan Cadet Corps Support Fund. The *www.fsk.ru*

Alexander Zhmodkov *Russian Cadet Corps www.napolean-series.org*

Battle of Vienna *www.wien-vienna.com*

October Revolution *Wikipedia*

http://en.wikipedia.org/wiki/October_Revolution

Polish – Russian War and Fight for Polish Independence, 1918-21 (Also known as the Russo-Polish War 1920) *by A. Mongeon*

http://home.golden.net/~medals/1918-1921.htm

Karalkapak *owned by David and Sue Richardson*

www.karalkapak.com

Russian Revolution. The *www.barnsdle.co.uk*

Russian Revolution 1917 *www.spartacus.school*

Map
http://en.wikipedia.org/wiki/file:Curzon_line_en.svg
Creative Commons Attribution – Share Alike 3.0 Unported licence